The Second Chafing Dish Cookbook

by Marie Roberson Hamm

Prentice-Hall Inc., Englewood Cliffs, N.J.

Fourth printing, June, 1967

The Second Chafing Dish Cookbook, by Marie Roberson Hamm
© 1963 by Prentice-Hall, Inc., Englewood Cliffs, N. J.

Library of Congress Catalog Card Number: 63-16736
79734-T

Contents

Foreword

The art of chafing dish cookery is for the happy-hearted, for the adventurous, for people in love. It is the darling of sophisticated chefs. This sort of on-stage cooking appeals to the hostess with a gift for imaginative hospitality, to the host who appreciates the minor splendors of life. A chafing dish is certainly a gourmet's best friend. With proper understanding of its utility, it can be your party-perfect servant.

Even if you are one of the fortunate few with a maid standing by, it is a double compliment to your guests, that you do the cooking yourself before their eyes. Be prepared for admiration as you add a dash of this, a cup of that. Why, the performance may even bring applause and flowers! It will certainly bring to you the satisfaction of serving in a graceful, interesting, and different way.

I can promise, if you follow carefully the recipes you find in these pages, that the results will outshine the performance.

From the dish's shining depths will arise appetizing perfumes to shame those of Araby, and foods seasoned with a full measure of enchantment. You'll find it queen of the buffet, king of the cocktail hour. I urge you to employ your chafing dish at every opportunity; to enjoy a new ease of cooking as you chat with friends (what a blow to kitchen servitude); and to reflect in the sparkle it adds to occasions, large and small.

Since publication of *The Chafing Dish Cookbook* thirteen years ago, and of the *Revised and Enlarged Version,* which appeared eight years later, I have been collecting recipes from generous and helpful sources all over the world. These have been cooked and served, much to the delight of my guests and my husband, Fred, in elegant chafing dish fashion. And so, gradually the *Second Chafing Dish Cookbook* has come about, not through toil, but through a delightful series of delicious adventures.

Nothing nourishes the egos of actors, authors, and publishers alike as the words "Bravo, encore!" Heartening requests from a large and enthusiastic audience have confirmed the need for this book of entirely new recipes as a companion to its first-born sibling, a perennial classic now in its twelfth printing (70,000 copies) and still showing splendid vitality.

We wish to thank those readers who have thrown us a legacy of kudos for their enthusiasm and encouragement.

Bon Appetit!

MARIE ROBERSON HAMM

Introduction

Where or When, Dear Chafing Dish?
When is around the clock.
Where is indoors, outdoors, and all around the town.

Your chafing dish is the most portable cooking unit that exists. I heard of a man who carried one with him on a trip around the world because he wanted his breakfast kidneys cooked in just a certain way. So you can visualize its usefulness at the next meeting of your club or church supper. In grandmother's day, it was a popular unit in every young lady's college room, and it has returned to enjoy that happy young distinction again. When the teen group plan a "mixer," the chafing dish is for them. Perhaps the master of the house is having a stag supper on poker night—bring out your favorite dish, and he'll have a hit on his hands (men love chafing dish service).

Keep it in mind when you're eating outdoors too. It reigns supreme on the patio where hot foods are apt to cool off in a hurry. If a high breeze is blowing, fashion a small screen of cardboard to protect the flame.

Cocktail parties take on added romance when a chafing dish offers piping hot snacks. After football games or winter sports your chafing dish will radiate physical warmth and fuel for the inner man from its hospitable bowl. Buffet tables seem meager and cheerless without chafing dish service, and Open House Parties are lame without its shining presence. In fact, it is often said that the traditional open house exists because of the chafing dish. And please don't forget this faithful servant when you plan a committee meeting, a tea, or a wedding reception.

A California friend cherishes her dish as part of a Sunday ceremony. She asks friends as she leaves church to stop by for a cup of hot soup and a snack on the way home, a charming custom that should be encouraged everywhere.

IT'S SO EASY!

A chafing dish is the most versatile "stove" for specialty cooking; it is completely portable and ready for use at a moment's notice. To be an accomplished chafing dish operator requires nothing more than confidence, a little courage at first, patience to follow step-by-step instructions, and a sense of timing (native to any good cook) for adding spices, liquors, and other ingredients at the proper moment.

Even though modern kitchens grow more beautifully efficient every year, the hostess yearns to be with her guests when they come to call. And a chafing dish allows her to enjoy the fun while she prepares exotic dishes with unhurried step-saving ease at the living room or dining room table in their presence. It can all be done with even less trouble than at a kitchen range. The reason is simple—all ingredients are measured and tray-ready for use within her reach.

In this modern day the average person is cook, waitress, and hostess in one package. Entertaining is difficult unless plans are preconceived. The strategy, simple like any successfully designed campaign, is merely a set of time-saving rules:

1. Market the day before.
2. Fill ice bucket early in the day and make new ice.
3. Arrange table setting and centerpiece.
4. Lay out linen, silver, china, glass.
5. Prepare ahead as much food as possible.
6. Make cocktails ahead and offer choice of two.
7. Limit menu to three courses, such as main dish, salaa, dessert.

Now, you can relax and enjoy the leisurely delights with your friends.

The Ritual

Chafing dish cooking creates an atmosphere of elegant informality and intimacy. The food bubbling in the dish will bring a warm glow of contentment to the most exacting guests. Soft music can add much to the mood.

The tray of ingredients should be attractively set with smart containers. Use your handsomest serving forks and spoons. A wire whisk, when needed, will add to the sophisticated array. Matched salt and pepper mills lend the tray the air of a succulent still life.

Since you are the star of the drama, confidence is your cue. Step to the center of the stage and light the flame. You're on! Make the most of every minute. Relax and operate with calm efficiency.

You've already checked the fuel supply and double-checked the ingredient tray, so you know they're under control. Keep the recipe close by, following each step with care. Now you're on the high road of culinary eminence enjoyed by those master chefs of chafing dish cooking, the Maître d's of the world's finest restaurants.

If you are preparing a flaming dish, add a touch of genius by darkening the room. The only light will be the flickering flame of the burner. Then, a match to the volatile liquor, whoosh, and the room is alight with the subtle blue flame of the dish.

Voilà! The preparation is completed, and your fascinated guests hover at your shoulder murmuring sounds of admiration. Warm plates stand near. The food is served, and the murmurs turn to shouts of praise—your hour has arrived!

How to Recognize a Chafing Dish Recipe

Many of your favorite recipes can be converted to chafing dish use. Once you get the knack of using your "parlor stove," you'll be quick to recognize those which are adaptable if you keep these easy rules in mind.

Remember that this type of cooking is similar to top-of-stove and double-boiler cooking; however, the heat is less flexible. If you use Sterno fuel, it will in all probability take longer, as you will be cooking on low. Regard an alcohol flame as medium heat and a candle-warmer, as its name implies, as merely a utensil to keep food warm.

Dishes That May Be "In"	Dishes That Are "Out"
Short cooking	Long cooking
Low or medium heat	Oven
Skillet	Broiler
Saucepan	Blender or shaker
Double-boiler	Refrigerator
Flaming	Large quantity
Two-quarts or less	

Examples

A creamy tuna dish which could be prepared in a saucepan over low heat is a good bet, while a tuna-noodle oven casserole is not.

A custard that needs baking in the oven would never do, but a Zabaglione-type custard that can be stirred over water until thick would make a fine chafing dish recipe.

Roast meats are naturally eliminated, but hamburgers and many quick-cooking chopped, diced, or canned meats that are usually cooked in a skillet the size of your chafing dish pan would be logical.

Stews that require hours of cooking are not members of the chafing dish family, but quicker-cooking beef Stroganoff or veal kidneys in wine sauce are great chafing dish specialties. Reasonably, a stew, which is generally served in large helpings, would be too massive for large group servings.

Steaks or chops that require direct overhead heat are not serious contenders for chafing dish cookery. Thin cuts of tender meat such as filet mignon, liver, or veal scaloppine that require more rapid skillet-cooking are very much in the running.

Cheese and egg dishes that do not need oven heat are the natural champions of chafing dish cookery; saucy meats, such as creamed chipped beef, curries, and à la king-type dishes, are other Main Course specialties.

Hot desserts, heated in sauce, especially the lovely desserts with wine or brandy, often gloriously blazing, are the showiest and most applauded of the whole family—and why not? They ring down the curtain of a pleasurable meal.

YOUR CHAFING DISH KEEPS FOOD HOT, TOO

Lack of knowledge constricts the use of many perfectly good chafing dishes to simple service as food warmers. This is, of course, as belittling as a full general being mistaken for the doorman at the Roxy. However, I must admit that there have been many instances in my hostess life when I have cooked dishes ahead and served them with dash and dazzle from my chafing dish, some of the recipes in this very book, to be truthful.

When there are limits to the allotted cooking time, when certain circumstances prevent the tableau of chafing dish cooking—whatever the reason—all of these recipes, and others that fall in the chafing dish league, will be at home served in your elegant "parlor serving stove."

PARTIAL CHAFING DISH COOKING

At other times you may find it more convenient to partially cook the food in advance and finish the preparation before your guests; for example, the length of time required to cook Bavarian Pork Chops on page 73 might be impractical. So, in your leisure time, either over the chafing dish flame or on your kitchen range, brown the chops in the blazer pan, cover, and simmer for 30 minutes. Just before serving, place the uncovered blazer pan over the chafing dish flame and cook until the pan juices are reduced to half; then proceed with the applejack flaming according to the recipe.

THE CLASSIC CHAFING DISH

The most familiar and practical chafing dish is a light, portable metal cooking unit set in a stand with a burner at the bottom. The stand supports a water pan and a blazer pan with a lid. The burner, recessed in a chamber directly beneath the pans, provides the heat.

The fuels used are usually Sterno or alcohol. The heat is controlled by a moveable lid attached to the fuel container which can be adjusted to allow wide or narrow flame exposures. When closed altogether it extinguishes the flame. Canned Sterno heat comes in two sizes, and, of course, if your dish can accommodate the larger can, you will find that it provides the greater heat. Alcohol has more intense heat than Sterno; it is also more tricky to use. If not handled with respect, alcohol heat has some elements of danger. Sterno is the safer of the two; alcohol is the least expensive.

Electric chafing dishes are similar to electric skillets and should always come with complete instructions. While they are convenient, easy, and inexpensive to use, the cooking control is less flexible, since the coils hold their heat for a while. An asbestos pad can be used as protection from too much heat, or you can remove the pan from the heat until the coils cool to desired heat.

Since the heating power of chafing dishes varies considerably, the cooking times for these recipes are necessarily approximate. And, to reiterate, when the cooking time for a recipe is lengthy and your chafing dish is one of minor heating strength, it is sometimes wise to start the preparation on your kitchen range before guests arrive and do the showy finishing touches "before the eyes."

The water pan is used in the same capacity as the bottom of a double boiler. The layer of boiling or simmering water between the heat and the food provides the gentlest kind of cooking, regulating the preparation of creamy sauces and other delicate mixtures which might scorch or curdle in direct contact with heat. Not much water is needed in the bottom pan. In fact, about three quarters to one inch will suffice, with more added if necessary over a long period of time. Too much water will bubble over as it boils. The double-boiler arrangement also allows you to keep foods hot for some time without overcooking. To save time, have the water boiling before you pour it into the water pan.

You may use the upper dish without the water pan in the manner of a skillet or saucepan for frying, sautéing, or simmering. It is excellent for quick medium to high heat cooking and for flaming. You will note that the bulk of the recipes in this book require the blazer pan without a water pan.

The most popular dishes have a 2-quart capacity. They are made of copper, stainless steel, aluminum, or silver plate, and sometimes of earthenware. The copper dishes are lined with tin or silver plate and prove very effective because copper is an excellent conductor of heat. However, the tin plate can be quickly worn through if the following precautions are not observed. Use wooden forks and spoons which will not scratch or damage the tin lining. Use only soap and water or the mildest cleaning powders to prolong the life of the plating.

RELATIVES OF THE CHAFING DISH FAMILY

CRÊPE PAN

This pan is the one you have admired in fashionable restaurants. It is the darling of the great Maître d's—the instrument of their most rewarding masterpieces, the flaming crêpe suzette. The crêpe pan can be awkwardly used on your burner-stand, but to use it correctly, you should cook the tiny pancakes over the standard equipment of the restaurant world, the réchauld burner, a handy flame-shielded stove with a handle and an adjustable heat container. The crêpe equipment can be used for a limited number of other dishes, so unless you intend to specialize in crêpes, it is an expensive addition to your culinary appointments. Actually, while it is a bit clumsy because of the deep sides, your chafing dish can prepare crêpes that taste just as delicious.

FONDUE DISH

The Swiss have an affectionate name, "fondue," for their favorite party dish. There are several varieties of this do-it-yourself dinner, mainly cheese and meat, but the method of eating is its unorthodox feature. Each member of the group sticks long forks into the pot and then pops the speared tidbits into his mouth. The cooking apparatus is an earthenware or heat-proof porcelain casserole which sits on a stand over a flame; however, the traditional equipment can be replaced by your all-purpose chafing dish.

PETITE MARMITE

French as bouillabaisse and the proper "cooker" for this famous one-dish specialty is the petite marmite, a deep crockery casserole of large size which holds four to six quarts. It is supported by a substantial burner-stand and is primarily used for soups, marmites, and stews. Again, unless you entertain in a large and informal way and have frequent use for such restaurant-type paraphernalia, the gross proportions of the petite marmite are unwieldly for most households.

WARMERS

Warming dishes and candle warmer-casserole combinations have a definite place in modern life but need no explaining, since we see them in use so frequently. The principle is simply placing heat beneath cooked food to keep it hot.

TRAY-MAID

You're setting the stage with subtle excitement for a romantic adventure with good food, soft music, and wine. Appetizing showmanship is your cue. It must be approached in an orderly manner. Candlelight is ideal, if you can amass sufficient tapers for the task at hand. If not, fall back on that ubiquitous utility, electric light.

The most important element in rousing appetites and keeping them roused is the beauty of the raw ingredients on the tray.

Now, step back into the kitchen and consider how this can be done. First, choose a tray that will, in size and color, do full justice to the dish you're chafing. If you have a choice of small dishes, select a happy contrast for the ingredients that you will be using. Suppose that your Duck-a-Tash (page 93) tray-maid ingredients are cheddar-cheese soup, cream, cubed duck, succotash, pimiento, sherry, and toast points. You might use a black tray and these containers: a large glass measuring cup for the soup; a set of matched blue cups for the cream, pimiento, and sherry; small red mixing bowls for the duck and succotash; and a basket with a yellow napkin for the toast points.

Neat preparation of the materials (precise slicing, cubing, shredding, and so forth) will increase the order and beauty in the eye of your audience. Handsome pepper mills always strike a dramatic note. They always exercise the enormous one in elegant restaurants.

Check the contents of the Tray-Maid list again before taking it on the set. Do you have each item? Are there any additional ingredients that you may want for your own original version? All set? Then, start cooking.

But, please, don't nervously dispatch all those carefully arranged ingredients, plunk, into the chafing dish. With a tender hand, graciously add them, one at a time, not for showmanship alone, but also for goodness of flavor and texture. Stir with affection until the dish has "arrived." Then continue the artistic technique as each serving is arranged on the plates.

HERE'S HOW!

To achieve a rich brown on meats or in gravies use a gravy coloring agent such as Kitchen Bouquet, Maggi, or Gravy Secret.

To develop a crisp crust on patties, croquettes, and the like, roll them in bread or cracker crumbs rather than flour.

To beautify a creamed dish, such as an à la king, a stew, or a curry, reserve some of the most eye-appealing ingredients and use them as a garnish. If this is not possible, add a sprinkling of chopped parsley, grated carrot, or sliced stuffed olives for the cordon bleu touch.

To add crunch to the menu, serve crusty hot breads or fresh toast. Crisp salads served before or with the main dish are always welcome texture contrast to creamy foods.

To arrest the appetites of those driven to the verge of drooling madness, pour demi-tasse cups of consommé as a "waiting beverage" to hold them in check while you cook.

To flame, use good liquors to get the best residual effect. The purpose of flaming is to burn off the alcohol and retain the flavor. Before igniting, warm the liquor (or liqueur) in a pipkin or ladle. Then set it afire either before or after pouring it on the food, but do not light it until the sulphurous head of the match has burned away. Incidentally, do not pour *from a bottle* into a hot pan; the bottle could explode!

To complete the mood of the meal, serve goblets of sparkling dry wine; red with meat and white with poultry or fish is the general rule, but not the law.

1.

Hot
Cocktail Tidbits
Rate Raves

No cold cardboard pasties these! but, crisp and succulent nuggets of piping-hot compelling savor. Watch the "action" as your guests forget liquid refreshments in their rush to the hors d'oeuvre corner. Armed with toothpicks and napkins they'll joust for the last Triangle Diablo or Oyster Wrap-Up. Here are rare sops for bottled spirits, to keep tongues witty with fluid conversation.

1

DRIED BEEF SURPRISE

1 pound cream cheese
1½ cups chopped salted nuts
1 tablespoon Worcestershire sauce
dash freshly ground pepper
16-20 pieces of dried beef
2 tablespoons butter

Beforehand   Soften cream cheese and blend in nuts and seasonings. Form into 16-20 balls depending on the size desired. Place a ball in the center of each piece of dried beef and roll. It is not necessary to soak the beef because the salt will give a nice flavor to the cheese. Tuck in the ends of the beef and secure each roll with a pick.

Tray-Maid   Prepared dried beef rolls, and butter.

On Stage   Melt butter in blazer pan of chafing dish until it sizzles. Sauté rolls in butter until browned on all sides. Serve hot with picks.

BALONEY BOATS WITH CAPERED EGG SALAD

4 hard-cooked eggs	2 tablespoons mayonnaise
1 teaspoon salt	1 tablespoon capers
½ teaspoon white pepper	12 slices baloney
½ teaspoon dry mustard	2 tablespoons butter

Beforehand Dice hard-cooked eggs and blend with salt, pepper, dry mustard, mayonnaise and capers. Set aside to chill.

Tray-Maid Bowl of prepared egg salad, slices of baloney, and butter.

On Stage Melt butter in blazer pan of chafing dish until it sizzles. Sauté baloney in butter until they curl up and form cups. Let guests fill their own baloney boats with the egg salad.

TRIANGLES DIABLO

12 slices day-old bread
3 eggs
2 cups milk
1 teaspoon chili powder
1 teaspoon salt
dash cayenne pepper
4 tablespoons butter

DIAVOCADO SPREAD

1 large ripe avocado, mashed
2 tablespoons lemon juice
1 tablespoon mayonnaise
1 teaspoon chili powder
½ teaspoon salt
⅛ teaspoon garlic powder
dash cayenne pepper

Beforehand Remove crusts from bread and cut on the diagonal to form triangles. Beat eggs and add milk and seasonings. Blend well. Mix all spread ingredients until well blended and chill. Just before preparing food, dip each triangle quickly in the egg-milk mixture.

Tray-Maid Prepared triangles, butter, and Diavocado spread.

On Stage Melt butter in blazer pan of chafing dish until it sizzles. Sauté triangles in butter until browned on both sides. It may be necessary to add more butter to the pan to brown all the bread. To serve, let guests spread the triangles with the spread.

MINIATURE CABBAGE BUNDLES

1 head cabbage (about 1½ pounds)	3 tablespoons chili sauce
2 cups cooked rice	1 teaspoon salt
1 pound ground round steak	¼ teaspoon pepper
1 small onion minced	dash Tabasco
½ cup sour cream	1 10½-ounce can condensed consommé

Beforehand Pour boiling water over cabbage and let stand 5 minutes. Drain and carefully remove the leaves. Cut out the heavy thick rib of the larger outer leaves. Cut the larger leaves in half. Remove enough leaves to make 16 bundles. It may be necessary to pour additional boiling water over cabbage to remove the inner leaves. Mix rice, beef, onion, and sour cream. Blend in chili sauce and seasonings. Form into 16 mounds and place each mound in the center of a wilted leaf. Roll carefully, turning in the ends to the center to make 16 bundles. Secure well with picks.

Tray-Maid Prepared cabbage bundles and consommé.

On Stage Heat consommé in blazer pan of chafing dish until it comes to a gentle boil. Carefully arrange the bundles in the hot consommé. Cover and simmer 15 minutes, turning occasionally to cook all sides. Remove cover and cook 10 minutes longer. Keep hot over hot water.

SAVORY CHICKEN BALLS

1½ cups cooked chicken
¼ cup India relish, well drained
1 egg, beaten
⅓ cup fine dry bread crumbs
¼ teaspoon curry powder

¼ teaspoon salt
dash cayenne pepper
½ cup fine cheese-cracker
  crumbs
2 tablespoons butter

Beforehand   Grind chicken and mix with all remaining ingredients except cracker crumbs and butter. Form into 1-inch balls. Roll balls in crumbs. Refrigerate until needed.

Tray-Maid   Prepared chicken balls and butter.

On Stage   Heat butter in blazer pan of chafing dish until it sizzles. Sauté balls in butter until lightly browned. Serve with picks. Makes 18-20 balls.

CHICKEN LIVERS AND MUSHROOMS IN WINE SAUCE

1 pound chicken livers
1 cup fine dry bread crumbs
1 teaspoon celery salt
1 teaspoon salt
½ teaspoon freshly ground pepper

2 3-ounce cans button mushrooms
3 tablespoons butter
1 cup chicken broth
½ cup California dry sherry

Beforehand Wash, drain, and cut chicken livers in half. Place bread crumbs and seasonings in a paper bag and toss livers in mixture until lightly coated. Drain mushrooms.

Tray-Maid Prepared chicken livers, mushrooms, butter, broth, and sherry.

On Stage Melt butter in blazer pan of chafing dish until it sizzles. Sauté livers 8-10 minutes in butter until browned and just done (the redness will disappear). Add mushrooms and broth. Heat to simmering, stirring up the brown specks in the bottom of the pan. Pour wine over and heat again just to simmering. Serve with picks.

HONG KONG CHICKEN LIVERS

1 clove garlic
1 pound chicken livers
2 tablespoons butter
1 teaspoon soy sauce
2 tablespoons finely chopped parsley
Melba toast rounds

Beforehand   Peel and split clove of garlic. Wash chicken livers and drain well. Heat Melba toast rounds.

Tray-Maid   Garlic, drained chicken livers, butter, soy sauce, parsley, and hot Melba toast rounds.

On Stage   Rub blazer pan of chafing dish with clove of garlic. Melt butter in the pan until it sizzles. Sauté chicken livers in butter until browned on all sides (about 10 minutes or until the redness disappears). Add soy sauce and stir gently to mix. Just before serving sprinkle with parsley. Keep warm over hot water. Serve with picks and hot Melba toast rounds.

CRAB MEAT PATTIES

⅔ cup cocktail sauce
1 egg
1 cup fine dry bread crumbs
1 teaspoon seasoned salt
½ teaspoon seasoned pepper
1 teaspoon finely chopped
　parsley
1 teaspoon finely chopped
　green onions

1 6½-ounce can crab meat
1 teaspoon lemon juice
1 egg (for dipping)
1 cup (about) fine dry bread
　crumbs for dipping
3 tablespoons butter
2 dozen saltines

Beforehand　Combine all ingredients except egg and crumbs for dipping, butter, and saltines. Mix thoroughly and form mixture into about 24 small flat patties. Dip in egg and then coat with bread crumbs. Refrigerate until needed. Just before starting, toast the saltines and keep them warm.

Tray-Maid　Prepared crab meat patties, butter, and toasted saltines.

On Stage　Melt butter in blazer pan of chafing dish until it sizzles. Sauté patties in butter until golden brown on both sides. Keep warm over hot water. Serve with toasted saltines.

SAUCY DEVILED EGGS

8 hard-cooked eggs
1 3-ounce can deviled ham
3 tablespoons chopped black olives
2 tablespoons heavy cream
dash cayenne pepper
2 tablespoons butter

3 tablespoons finely chopped green onion
1 teaspoon salt
1 teaspoon celery seed
½ teaspoon sugar
2 8-ounce cans tomato sauce
16 slices oblong rye Melba toast

Beforehand Cut eggs in half and remove yolks. For a smooth mixture force yolks through a sieve. Blend yolks with ham, olives, cream, and pepper. Fill egg-white halves with yolk mixture. Mix onion with seasonings.

Tray-Maid Deviled eggs, butter, seasoned onions, tomato sauce, and Melba toast.

On Stage Melt butter in blazer pan of chafing dish until sizzling. Cook onion in butter until limp but still green. Pour in tomato sauce. Cover and simmer 10 minutes. Remove cover and place egg halves in sauce. Drizzle some of sauce over each egg. Cover and simmer 5 minutes longer. Keep warm over hot water. Serve on Melba toast.

FRANKFURTER PENNIES

1 bay leaf	2 tablespoons vinegar
1 teaspoon whole cloves	2 tablespoons brown sugar
1 teaspoon peppercorns	1 teaspoon salt
2 cups tomato juice	8 skinless frankfurters
½ cup chili sauce	

Beforehand   Tie bay leaf, whole cloves and peppercorns in a small piece of cheesecloth. Add to juice mixed with all remaining ingredients except frankfurters. Simmer, uncovered, 15 minutes. Cool, cover, and refrigerate. Just before starting, remove bag of spices from juice and cut frankfurters into pennies.

Tray-Maid   Prepared barbecue sauce and sliced frankfurters.

On Stage   Heat sauce in blazer pan of chafing dish until it bubbles. Add frankfurter pennies and simmer until heated through. Keep warm over hot water. Makes about 50 pennies.

CRUNCHY GARLIC LIVERWURST BALLS

1½ pounds liverwurst (plain or
  smoked)
2 tablespoons finely minced
  green onion
2 tablespoons very finely minced parsley
20-24 garlic croutons
butter

Beforehand   Remove skin from liverwurst and let stand at
room temperature to soften. When soft, cream in onion
and parsley. Divide mixture into 20-24 balls. Place a crouton
in the center of each liverwurst ball and cover well. Chill.

Tray-Maid   Liverwurst balls and butter.

On Stage   Heat enough butter in blazer pan of chafing dish
to evenly cover the bottom. When butter sizzles, add balls,
a few at a time, and sauté until lightly browned on all sides.
Keep hot over hot water. Serve with picks. The balls are
very good because of the contrast between the meat covering and the crisp crouton.

ONE-BITE MEAT BALLS IN DILL SAUCE

1¼ pounds ground round steak

4 tablespoons fine dry rye-bread crumbs

1 teaspoon salt

½ teaspoon monosodium glutamate

2 tablespoons ketchup

3 tablespoons butter

2 tablespoons flour

½ teaspoon celery salt

1 10½-ounce can condensed consommé

1 tablespoon finely chopped fresh dill or 2 teaspoons dried powdered dill

Beforehand Mix beef, bread crumbs, salt, monosodium glutamate, and ketchup. Form mixture into about 48 1-inch balls. Refrigerate until needed. Combine flour and celery salt.

Tray-Maid Prepared meat balls, butter, flour mixed with celery salt, consommé, and dill.

On Stage Melt butter in blazer pan of chafing dish until it sizzles. Add meat balls, a few at a time, browning on all sides. As meat balls brown remove from the pan and add others until all are browned. Keep them warm in a covered dish. Blend flour mixture into butter remaining in the pan. Cook, stirring constantly until smooth. Gradually stir in consommé and cook 6-8 minutes until thickened. Add dill and meat balls. Mix well. Cover and keep warm over hot water. Serve with picks.

HOT DEVILED MUSHROOM ROUNDS

1 tablespoon butter
1 tablespoon flour
¼ teaspoon salt
dash freshly ground pepper
2 tablespoons heavy cream
1 3-ounce can broiled mushrooms

¼ cup grated sharp cheddar cheese
18 slices thin white bread cut in rounds
1 3-ounce can deviled tongue

Beforehand   Blend flour with seasonings. Measure cream and mix with liquid drained from mushrooms. Chop mushrooms. Toast bread rounds, spread them with tongue, and keep them hot.

Tray-Maid   Butter, seasoned flour, cream-mushroom liquid, chopped mushrooms, grated cheese, and toasted rounds spread with tongue.

On Stage   Melt butter in blazer pan of chafing dish. Blend in seasoned flour, mixing until smooth. Gradually blend in cream-mushroom liquid. Cook, stirring constantly until thickened. Add mushrooms and cheese. Stir until cheese melts. Keep warm over hot water. Pile on the toast rounds.

BLUSHING MUSHROOMS

2 3-ounce cans whole button mushrooms	1 teaspoon flour
	1 teaspoon paprika
2 tablespoons butter	½ teaspoon salt
1 teaspoon lemon juice	dash white pepper
2 tablespoons finely chopped chives	¼ cup sour cream

Beforehand Drain mushrooms. Mix chives, flour, paprika, salt, and pepper together to avoid having too many little piles of ingredients.

Tray-Maid Butter, drained mushrooms, lemon juice, mixed dry ingredients, and sour cream.

On Stage Heat butter in blazer pan of chafing dish until it sizzles. Sauté mushrooms in butter until lightly browned, (about 5-8 minutes). Stir in lemon juice. Sprinkle dry ingredients over. Mix until mushrooms are well blended and mixture is smooth. Add sour cream. Blend well. Keep hot over hot water. Serve with picks.

STUFFED MUSHROOM MEDLEY

12 large mushrooms	⅓ cup dry bread crumbs
½ cup consommé	2 tablespoons finely minced pimiento
¼ teaspoon garlic salt	
dash cayenne pepper	3 tablespoons butter

Beforehand   Remove stems and scoop out centers of mushrooms to form a hollow cap. Mince the stems and scooped out pieces and cook in consommé until tender (about 5 minutes). Drain liquid and reserve. Mix together drained mushroom pieces, seasonings, bread crumbs, and pimiento.

Tray-Maid   Prepared mushroom stuffing, mushroom caps, butter, and reserved mushroom liquid.

On Stage   Heat butter in blazer pan of chafing dish until it sizzles. Sauté mushroom caps in butter for 5 minutes. Turn rounded sides down and fill each hollow with stuffing. Sprinkle with reserved mushroom liquid. Cover and simmer, basting occasionally with pan juices until heated through. Serve with picks.

More Stuffings   Omit pimiento and add 1 tablespoon finely chopped chives and 1 tablespoon chopped parsley to bread crumb mixture. Omit pimiento and add 3 tablespoons finely chopped salted pecans. Omit pimiento and add 3 tablespoons finely chopped ripe olives to the bread crumb mixture.

HOT DEVILED NUTS

½ pound shelled almonds	3 tablespoons butter
½ pound shelled pecans	2 teaspoons chili powder
½ pound shelled filberts	2 teaspoons seasoned salt
¼ cup salad oil	1 teaspoon seasoned pepper

Beforehand Blanch almonds by dipping in hot water for a few minutes. Remove from water and cool. Slip off the skins and dry thoroughly. Mix with the other nuts. Mix seasonings.

Tray-Maid Nuts, oil, butter, and seasonings.

On Stage Heat oil and butter in blazer pan of chafing dish until sizzling. Add nuts and seasonings. Sauté, stirring occasionally, until golden brown and well-covered with seasonings. Lower heat to keep hot and let guests help themselves.

BLACK BEAUTIES

24 pitted ripe olives, colossal size
8 wedges gruyère cheese
12 slices lean bacon

Beforehand Drain olives. Cut each wedge of cheese into 4 pieces, making 24 small wedges, and stuff each into an olive cavity. Cut bacon in half. Roll each olive in a piece of bacon, being sure to cover the cheese. Secure with a pick (a wooden one please).

Tray-Maid Bacon-wrapped olives.

On Stage Heat blazer pan of chafing dish until a drop of water sizzles when dropped into it. Sauté bacon-wrapped olives, turning occasionally until browned and bacon is crisp. Drain off excess fat.

CRUNCHY OYSTERS

2 cans smoked oysters
2 tablespoons bacon or ham drippings
3 tablespoons sesame seeds
½ teaspoon paprika

Beforehand Drain oysters well. Measure bacon or ham drippings. Butter may be used but bacon fat gives an interesting flavor to the oysters. Mix sesame seeds and paprika.

Tray-Maid Oysters, bacon drippings, and sesame seed mixture.

On Stage Melt drippings until sizzling in blazer pan of chafing dish. Sauté oysters until just heated through (about 5 minutes). Drain off excess fat. Sprinkle with sesame seed mixture. Keep warm over hot water. Serve with picks.

OYSTER WRAP-UPS

2 dozen oysters*   1 teaspoon salt
½ cup prepared cocktail sauce   ¼ teaspoon seasoned pepper
1 tablespoon horseradish   12 slices lean bacon
1 tablespoon tarragon vinegar   sesame Melba toast rounds
few drops Tabasco sauce

Beforehand   Drain oysters of all liquid, reserving 1 cup. Mix oyster liquid with cocktail sauce, horseradish, vinegar, and seasonings. Pour mixture over oysters, cover, and let stand in refrigerator for several hours to season and mellow the flavor. Cut bacon in half. Just before cooking, drain oysters and wrap each in bacon. Secure with a pick.

Tray-Maid   Bacon-wrapped oysters and sesame Melba toast rounds.

On Stage   Heat blazer pan of chafing dish until piping hot. (A drop of water will sputter when dropped into the pan.) Place bacon-wrapped oysters in pan and sauté until evenly browned on all sides and bacon is crisp. Spoon out excess bacon drippings. Keep hot or cook a few at a time. Serve with sesame Melba toast rounds.

* Scallops or shrimp may also be used in place of the oysters.

SPRIGGED SAUSAGE ROLLS

16 slices very fresh bread
¼ cup ketchup
16 brown-and-serve sausages
16 sprigs fresh parsley
3 tablespoons butter
1 clove garlic

Beforehand Remove crusts from bread. Spread each slice with ketchup. Place one sausage on each slice of bread and roll. Secure with a pick. Tuck a sprig of parsley in one end of each roll. Split clove of garlic.

Tray-Maid Sausage rolls, butter, and garlic.

On Stage Place butter and garlic in blazer pan of chafing dish. Heat until the butter sizzles. While the butter is heating, rub the garlic with a spoon on the bottom of the pan. Remove garlic. Sauté sausage rolls until browned on all sides. Keep warm over hot water. Serve with picks.

HOT TARTAR DIP FOR SEAFOOD TIDBITS

1 tablespoon butter
2 tablespoons flour
1 teaspoon salt
½ teaspoon seasoned pepper
¾ cup light cream
¼ cup butter
½ cup pickle relish

Beforehand   Mix flour, salt, and pepper.

Tray-Maid   Measured butter (both amounts), seasoned flour, cream, pickle relish, and assorted seafood tidbits for dipping.

On Stage   Melt 1 tablespoon butter in blazer pan of chafing dish. Blend in seasoned flour, mixing until smooth. Gradually stir in cream, mixing until well blended. Stir until mixture comes to a gentle boil. Add ¼ cup of butter, teaspoon by teaspoon, blending well after each addition. Add pickle relish. Keep warm over hot water. *Do not re-boil.* Serve as a dip for cooked shrimp, lobster, fish balls, fish sticks.

CRUNCHY SCALLOPS AND PICKLE KABOBS

1 quart bay scallops
water
1 teaspoon peppercorns
1 teaspoon salt
1 bay leaf
½ cup milk

1 cup finely crushed potato chips
¼ cup bacon drippings
small cubes pickled watermelon rind

Beforehand   Wash scallops and simmer in enough water to cover with peppercorns, salt, and bay leaf for 8-10 minutes or until just fork tender. Drain on paper toweling and dip in milk. Roll in the potato chip crumbs until well coated. Refrigerate until needed.

Tray-Maid   Cooked, drained, and crumbed scallops, bacon drippings, and watermelon rind.

On Stage   Melt drippings until sizzling in blazer pan of chafing dish. Sauté scallops in fat until browned on all sides. Keep warm over hot water. Let guests serve themselves to scallops and watermelon rind kabob-style.

SAUCY CALIFORNIA SHRIMP

2 pounds fresh shrimp **or** 2 packages frozen shrimp, thawed
4 tablespoons butter
1 teaspoon powdered dill
1 clove garlic, finely minced

½ teaspoon salt
¼ cup **California white wine or Chablis**
1 cup tomato ketchup
2 tablespoons finely chopped parsley

Beforehand Wash shrimp and remove shells and black veins. Refrigerate until ready to cook. Blend together dill, garlic, and salt. Combine wine and ketchup.

Tray-Maid Chilled shrimp, butter, seasonings, and wine and ketchup mixture. Snipped parsley.

On Stage Melt butter in blazer pan of chafing dish until it sizzles. Stir in seasonings and cook 1 minute. Add shrimp and sauté until they are just pink and firm (about 6 to 8 minutes). *Do not overcook, as this toughens the shrimp.* Pour over wine and ketchup mixture. Blend well. Heat just to the simmering point. Sprinkle with parsley. Keep warm over hot water. Serve with picks. Serves 8.

BARBECUED SHRIMP

⅓ cup vinegar
2 8-ounce cans tomato sauce
2 tablespoons brown sugar
1 teaspoon dry mustard
1 tablespoon Worcestershire sauce
1 clove garlic

1 teaspoon seasoned salt
½ teaspoon pepper
2 tablespoons chopped onion
1½ pounds cooked, deveined shrimp
2 tablespoons finely chopped parsley

Beforehand   The day before the party, combine all ingredients except shrimp and parsley. Cook uncovered for 15 minutes, stirring occasionally. Cool and refrigerate until needed.

Tray-Maid   Prepared barbecue sauce, prepared shrimp, and chopped parsley.

On Stage   Heat sauce in blazer pan of chafing dish. Add shrimp and heat gently, stirring carefully to cover all the shrimp. Just before serving, sprinkle with parsley for a fresh green look. Serve with picks. The number of shrimp you will have depends on the grade of shrimp purchased, such as small, medium, large, or fancy.

SWISS LETTUCE PACKETS

1 large head lettuce (Boston or Simpson)	3 tablespoons heavy cream
1 chicken bouillon cube	1 10½-ounce can condensed tomato soup
2 tablespoons hot water	¾ cup water
1 cup fine dry rye-bread crumbs	16 buttered toast squares
2 cups grated swiss cheese	

Beforehand Remove the core from lettuce and trim the outer leaves. Pour boiling water into the cavity left by removing the core. Let stand 2 minutes. Drain and carefully remove the leaves. Some of the larger leaves can be cut in half. Dissolve bouillon cube in 2 tablespoons hot water. Mix with all remaining ingredients except tomato soup and water. Divide mixture into 16 mounds and place each mound in the center of a leaf. Carefully roll the filled leaves, tucking in the ends. Secure with picks. Open the soup and mix with the water. Prepare toast squares and keep hot.

Tray-Maid Prepared lettuce packets, blended tomato soup and water, and buttered toast squares.

On Stage Heat tomato soup mixture in blazer pan of chafing dish until it comes to a gentle boil. Place the packets in the hot soup, cover, and simmer 10 minutes. Remove cover and simmer 5 minutes longer. Keep warm over hot water. Serve on buttered toast squares.

NIPPY TOMATO DUNK

¾ cup chili sauce
3 tablespoons lemon juice
1 teaspoon Worcestershire
1 teaspoon dry mustard
½ teaspoon curry powder

1 6-ounce roll smoke-flavored cheese
1 tablespoon butter
assorted crisp fresh vegetables for dipping

Beforehand Mix chili sauce, lemon juice, Worcestershire sauce, mustard, and curry powder. Let stand several hours to blend and mellow the flavors. Break cheese into small pieces. Prepare bite-size pieces of vegetables such as zucchini, cauliflower, turnips, carrots, cucumbers, and so forth for dipping. Chill until serving time.

Tray-Maid Chili sauce mixture, pieces of cheese, butter, and vegetables arranged on platter for serving.

On Stage Melt butter in blazer pan of chafing dish until it sizzles. Add cheese and stir until just melted. Gradually stir in chili sauce mixture, mixing until well blended.

2.

"Souper" Suppers

For little suppers of cozy companionship, soup meals are highly recommended. One of the most constant of life's pleasures, soup infects the company with warm comfort and laughter. To the harmony of the table, your chafing dish will add brilliant eloquence and produce bisques, chowders, and bouillons of unsurpassed delight.

CLAM STEW

1 quart clams
water
2 cups heavy cream
3 tablespoons butter
1 teaspoon celery salt
4 saltines, finely crushed
paprika

Beforehand Drain clams and measure juice. Run fingers through clams and remove any pieces of shell. If clams are large, cut them in half. To measured clam juice add enough water to make 2 cups. Just before starting, heat the cream.

Tray-Maid Cleaned, drained, and cut clams, clam-water mixture, heated cream, butter, celery salt, cracker crumbs, and paprika.

On Stage Place clams, clam liquor, hot cream, butter and celery salt in blazer pan of chafing dish. Heat to just a gentle boil or until the clams are just tender and edges curl. Stir in the cracker crumbs. Keep hot but do not boil. Serve sprinkled with paprika. Makes 4 to 6 servings.

◄§ MENU §►

Clam Stew
Pilot Biscuits
Avocado-Tomato Salad
Sponge Cake with Hot Butterscotch
Sauce and Almonds
Tea

LOBSTER STEW

2 tablespoons butter
3 tablespoons flour
1 teaspoon seasoned salt
½ teaspoon white pepper
2 cups light cream
2 6½-ounce cans lobster
¼ cup chopped parsley

Beforehand   Blend flour and seasonings. Flake lobster meat and remove the thin bony tissue.

Tray-Maid   Butter, seasoned flour, cream, flaked lobster meat, and parsley.

On Stage   Heat butter in blazer pan of chafing dish until it sizzles. Mix in seasoned flour until well blended. Gradually stir in cream. Cook, stirring constantly, until thickened and smooth (about 10-12 minutes). Add lobster meat and simmer 5 minutes longer. Just before serving, stir in parsley. Makes 4 servings.

⋖ MENU ⋗

Lobster Stew
Toasted Hard Rolls
Fresh Raw Vegetable Platter
Mincemeat Tarts
Demitasse

OYSTER-MUSHROOM SOUP

1 quart oysters
2 10½-ounce cans cream of
  mushroom soup
2 cups light cream

1 teaspoon salt
⅛ teaspoon white pepper
chopped parsley
toasted oysterettes

Beforehand   Drain and reserve oyster liquid. Clean and chop oysters. Blend salt and pepper. Just before starting, toast the oysterettes and keep them hot.

Tray-Maid   Chopped oysters, oyster liquid, cream, seasonings, parsley, and toasted oysterettes.

On Stage   Blend oysters, oyster liquid, and soup in blazer pan of chafing dish. Cook until mixture reaches a gentle boil (about 8-10 minutes). Stir in cream and seasonings and heat until mixture simmers. Serve hot sprinkled with parsley and oysterettes. Makes 4-6 servings.

⋙ MENU ⋘

Oyster-Mushroom Soup
Oysterettes
Crisp Vegetable Salad
Apple Pie   Cheese
Coffee

CAROLINA CRAB BISQUE

2 tablespoons butter	2 tablespoons chopped parsley
2 tablespoons flour	2 cups milk
1 teaspoon salt	2 cups light cream
⅛ teaspoon white pepper	1 6½-ounce can crab meat
dash powdered basil	paprika

Beforehand Blend flour and seasonings. Blend milk and cream and refrigerate until needed. Flake crab meat and remove the thin bony tissues.

Tray-Maid Butter, seasoned flour, parsley, milk-cream mixture, flaked crab meat, and paprika.

On Stage Melt butter in blazer pan of chafing dish. Stir in seasoned flour and parsley. Cook, stirring constantly, until mixtures bubbles. Gradually add milk-cream mixture. Cook, stirring constantly, until mixture thickens (about 10 minutes). Stir in crab meat and heat until mixture just simmers. Serve hot, sprinkled with paprika. Makes 4 servings.

◄§ MENU §►

Carolina Crab Bisque
Sesame Seed Toast Fingers
Jellied Fresh Vegetable Ring with Coleslaw Center
Spice Cake   Frosted Grapes
Tea

QUICK HADDOCK CHOWDER

½ pound salt pork
½ cup chopped onion
1 10¼-ounce can frozen potato
   soup
4 peppercorns

1 bay leaf
1 small carrot, chopped
1 stalk celery, chopped
4 cups milk
1 pound smoked haddock

Beforehand   Dice salt pork into small cubes. Open and thaw potato soup. Tie peppercorns, bay leaf, carrot, and celery, in a small piece of cheesecloth. Remove bones from haddock, if not filleted. Cut into cubes.

Tray-Maid   Diced salt pork, onion, soup, cloth bag of seasonings, milk, and boned and cubed haddock.

On Stage   Cook salt pork in blazer pan of chafing dish until crisp and brown. Remove from pan and keep hot. Sauté onion in the fat until tender but not browned. Add all remaining ingredients. Cover and simmer 25 minutes, or until the fish is tender. Remove bag of seasonings. Serve hot, sprinkled with hot salt pork cubes. Makes 4 servings.

⋖§   MENU   §⋗

Quick Haddock Chowder
Toast Triangles
Cranberry-Apple-Nut Jelly Mold
Butter Cookies
Coffee

CORN TUNA CHOWDER

4 strips lean bacon
1 medium onion, chopped
4 stalks celery, chopped
1 20-ounce can cream-style corn
1 7-ounce can tuna

4 cups milk
1½ teaspoons salt
⅛ teaspoon white pepper
popcorn (popped)
garlic

Beforehand Cut bacon into pieces. Drain and flake tuna. Mix salt and pepper.

Tray-Maid Diced bacon, onion, celery, cream-style corn, flaked tuna, milk, mixed seasonings, popcorn, and garlic.

On Stage Heat blazer pan of chafing dish until a drop of water sputters when dropped into it. Cook bacon until browned and crisp. Remove bacon and keep warm. Cook onion and celery in bacon drippings until tender but not browned. Add corn, tuna, milk, and seasonings. Heat until soup simmers (about 10 minutes). Just before serving, sprinkle with bacon and popcorn. Makes 4 servings.

Variations Omit bacon and sauté onion and celery in butter. Sprinkle with sesame seeds before serving. Omit tuna and substitute salmon or shrimp. Omit tuna and substitute dried beef cut into shreds.

◄§ MENU §►

Corn Tuna Chowder
Toasted Rye Party Bread
Cottage Cheese, Relish, Vegetable Stick Tray
Date and Nut Torte
Coffee

JIFFY SPIFFY CHEESE SOUP

1 10½-ounce can cream of chicken soup
1 10½-ounce can onion soup
2 soup cans light cream

1 cup diced sharp cheddar cheese
chopped chives
pilot crackers

Beforehand   Blend soups. Just before starting, toast crackers and keep them warm.

Tray-Maid   Blended soups, cream, diced cheese, chives, and toasted pilot crackers.

On Stage   Place soups in blazer pan of chafing dish. Gradually stir in cream. Heat until small bubbles appear around the edge of the soup. Stir in cheese. Heat until cheese is almost melted but not quite. This gives an interesting appearance. Serve hot, sprinkled with the chopped chives and pilot crackers. Makes 4 servings.

◆§   MENU   ◈◆

Jiffy Spiffy Cheese Soup
Toasted Pilot Crackers
Celery, Radishes, Pickles
Cherry Pie with Hard Sauce
Coffee

PINK AND GREEN CALICO BEEF SOUP

1 11¼-ounce can green pea soup
1 10½-ounce can cream of celery soup
2 soup cans light cream

1 package dried beef
¼ cup heavy cream
chopped chives
paprika

Beforehand Shred dried beef (do not soak). Whip heavy cream just before starting to prepare the soup.

Tray-Maid Pea and celery soups, light cream, shredded beef, heavy cream whipped, chives, and paprika.

On Stage Place pea soup in blazer pan of chafing dish. Gradually stir in celery soup and light cream until the mixture is smooth and well blended. Heat until simmering. Add dried beef and stir to blend. Heat again to simmering. Serve hot with a garnish of whipped cream, chives and paprika. Makes 4 servings.

⋅§ MENU ⸙

Pink and Green Calico Beef Soup
Assorted Cracker and Cheese Tray
Fresh Fruit
Coffee

MEAT BALL SOUP

1 pound ground round steak
4 tablespoons fine dry bread crumbs
1 teaspoon salt
1 teaspoon monosodium gluta-mate
1 teaspoon chili powder
¼ teaspoon pepper
¼ teaspoon onion powder

¼ cup water
2 tablespoons butter
2 18-ounce cans tomato juice
⅓ cup elbow macaroni, un-cooked
1 cup cooked mixed vegetables
2 teaspoons Worcestershire sauce
grated parmesan cheese

Beforehand   Mix beef, bread crumbs, salt, monosodium glutamate, chili powder, pepper, onion powder, and water. Form into about 20 small balls.

Tray-Maid   Prepared meat balls, butter, tomato juice, macaroni, mixed vegetables, Worcestershire sauce, and parmesan cheese.

On Stage   Heat butter to sizzling in blazer pan of chafing dish. Brown meat balls on all sides in butter. Add all remaining ingredients except cheese. Cover and simmer 25-30 minutes, or until macaroni is fork tender. Stir occasionally. Serve the soup hot with a sprinkling of cheese. Makes 4 servings.

◄§   MENU   §►

Meat Ball Soup
Garlic Bread
Butterscotch Cream Pie
Coffee

CHICKEN SALAD SOUP

1 cup thinly sliced celery
½ cup thinly sliced green onions
2 cups water
1 teaspoon salt
2 10½-ounce cans cream of chicken soup

1½ soup cans milk
1 cup diced cooked chicken
2 tomatoes
watercress

Beforehand   Cook sliced celery and onions in water with salt until tender-crisp (about 8-10 minutes). Drain and reserve liquid. Peel and dice tomatoes. Wash and chop ½ bunch watercress.

Tray-Maid   Cooked celery and onions, reserved celery liquid, chicken soup, milk, diced chicken, tomatoes, and watercress.

On Stage   Place cooked celery, onions, reserved celery water, chicken soup, and milk in blazer pan of chafing dish. Cover and heat until the mixture simmers. Add tomatoes and chicken and simmer until heated through. Serve hot, garnished with watercress. Makes 4 servings.

◄§   MENU   §►

Chicken Salad Soup
Minced Ham and Pickle Sandwiches
on Toasted Cheese Bread
Apple Brown Betty with Cream
Tea

HOLIDAY TURKEY SOUP

1 turkey frame	¼ cup sliced carrots
2 quarts water	¼ cup rice, uncooked
1 teaspoon salt	1 10½-ounce can cream of veg-
½ cup sliced celery	etable soup
½ cup sliced onion	pieces of turkey

Beforehand   The day before making the soup, strip turkey frame of all pieces and shreds of turkey and set aside. Place turkey frame, skin, and any bits of stuffing in a saucepan with water, salt, celery, onion, and carrots. Cover and simmer 2 hours. Cool, strain, and measure. There should be about 6 cups left. Refrigerate until needed. Open can of soup. Have turkey meat ready.

Tray-Maid   Turkey broth, rice, chicken soup, and turkey pieces.

On Stage   Place turkey broth and rice in blazer pan of chafing dish. Cover and simmer, stirring occasionally, until the rice is tender (about 20-25 minutes). Stir in soup and turkey. Blend well. Cover and simmer 10 minutes longer. Makes 4-6 servings.

·ᢒ   MENU   ᢣ·

Holiday Turkey Soup
Toasted Hard Rolls
Tossed Green Salad with Chopped Egg
Fruit Cake   Ice Cream
Coffee

JAPANESE WATERCRESS SOUP

2 cups finely diced cooked pork
⅓ cup soy sauce
2 10½-ounce cans beef broth
2 soup cans water
1 bunch watercress
water chestnuts

Beforehand Marinate pork in soy sauce for 2 hours, stirring occasionally to cover all the meat. Blend soup with water and set aside. Wash, clean, and chop watercress. Slice water chestnuts.

Tray-Maid Diced pork, diluted beef broth, watercress, and water chestnuts.

On Stage Place marinated pork in blazer pan of chafing dish. Add broth, cover, and bring to a gentle boil. Cook 15-20 minutes. Add watercress. Stir to blend and cook 5 minutes longer. Serve hot, garnished with slices of water chestnut. Makes 4-5 servings.

◆§ MENU §◆

Japanese Watercress Soup
Shrimps Tempura
Rice
Mandarin Oranges Sprinkled with Brandy
Tea   Macaroons

CHUCK WAGON SOUP

1 cup thinly sliced green onions	8 frankfurters (about 1 pound)
1 cup thinly sliced celery	1 tablespoon Worcestershire sauce
2 18-ounce cans tomato-vegetable juice	1½ teaspoons salt
2 1-pound cans baked beans	cheese crackers

Beforehand Force *one* can of baked beans through a sieve. Slice frankfurters. Just before starting, toast cheese crackers and keep them warm.

Tray-Maid Celery, onions, juice, sieved beans, whole beans, sliced frankfurters, seasonings, and toasted cheese crackers.

On Stage Place green onions, celery, tomato-vegetable juice, Worcestershire sauce, and salt in blazer pan of chafing dish. Mix well. Cover and simmer 15 minutes. Add sieved beans, whole beans, and frankfurters. Cover and simmer 10 minutes longer, stirring occasionally. Serve with toasted cheese crackers. Makes 4-6 servings.

❧ MENU ☙

Chuck Wagon Soup
Toasted Cheese Crackers
Fruit Filled Melon Halves
Iced Coffee

CALIFORNIA VALLEY SAUSAGE-LIMA SOUP

1 package brown-and-serve
   sausages
½ cup chopped onion
2 20-ounce cans dried lima
   beans

1 8-ounce can tomato sauce
2 10½-ounce cans beef bouillon
chili powder

Beforehand Slice sausages into ¼-inch pieces. Do not drain lima beans.

Tray-Maid Sliced sausages, onion, lima beans, tomato sauce, bouillon, and chili powder.

On Stage Sauté sausages and onion in blazer pan of chafing dish until onions are tender and sausage slices are lightly browned. Add all remaining ingredients. Cover and simmer 20-25 minutes. Serve hot, sprinkled generously with chili powder. Makes 4-6 servings.

◄§ MENU §►

California Valley Sausage-Lima Soup
Puffed Crackers
Tossed Green Salad
Frozen Apple Cream
Hazelnut Cookies
Coffee

AUTUMN SOUP

3 tablespoons butter
3 tablespoons flour
1 teaspoon salt
½ teaspoon onion powder

¼ teaspoon nutmeg
4 cups milk
1 20-ounce can pumpkin
garlic croutons

Beforehand   Mix flour, salt, onion powder, and nutmeg.

Tray-Maid   Butter, seasoned flour, milk, pumpkin, and garlic croutons.

On Stage   Melt butter in blazer pan of chafing dish. Blend in seasoned flour until smooth. Gradually stir in milk. Cook, stirring constantly, until thickened (about 10 minutes). Gradually stir in pumpkin, mixing until smooth. Heat until the soup comes to a gentle boil. Serve hot, sprinkled with croutons. Makes 4-6 servings.

❧ MENU ☙

Autumn Soup
Garlic Croutons
Egg Salad Sandwiches
Grape-Apple-Mint Coupé
Spiced Tea

GARDEN LEEK SOUP

1 bunch leeks
1 stalk celery
2 cups grated raw potato
2 large carrots, grated
¼ cup butter

1 quart milk
1 teaspoon salt
⅛ teaspoon white pepper
paprika

Beforehand   Blend salt and pepper. Wash leeks and celery and cut them into thin slices. Grate potatoes and keep them from turning black, by covering with cold water until ready to use. Just before starting to make the soup, drain potatoes and wring them dry in a piece of cheesecloth.

Tray-Maid   Prepared vegetables, butter, milk, blended salt and pepper, and paprika.

On Stage   Heat butter until it sizzles in blazer pan of chafing dish. Cook leeks and celery in hot butter until soft but not browned (about 10 minutes). Add drained potatoes, carrots, and milk. Cover and cook 20 minutes longer, stirring occasionally. Add seasoning. Stir to blend well. Serve hot with dash of paprika. Makes 4 servings.

◆§   MENU   §◆

Garden Leek Soup
Toasted Cheese-Bacon Sandwiches
Wine Jelly   Chocolate Filled Cookies
Coffee

NEAPOLITAN SPINACH SOUP

1½ pounds fresh spinach *or*
2 10-ounce packages frozen chopped spinach, thawed
2 10½-ounce cans beef broth
2 soup cans water
⅔ cup grated parmesan cheese

Beforehand   Wash, drain, and chop spinach, or separate thawed spinach.

Tray-Maid   Beef broth, water, spinach, and cheese.

On Stage   Place broth and water in blazer pan of chafing dish and bring to a boil. Add spinach and simmer, covered, for 15 minutes, or until spinach is just tender and still green. Add cheese and stir until cheese is just melted. Serve immediately, with additional cheese, if desired. Makes 4-6 servings.

⋇ MENU ⋇

Neapolitan Spinach Soup
Italian Bread Sticks
Individual Casseroles of Baked Macaroni
Stewed Fruit Compote in Wine   Italian Cookies
Demitasse with Lemon Peel

FRESH TOMATO BOUILLON

1 pound tomatoes
1 cup finely sliced scallions
½ cup finely chopped parsley
1 teaspoon monosodium glutamate

⅛ teaspoon pepper
¼ teaspoon sugar
3 10½-ounce cans beef broth
chopped fresh dill or powdered
   dill

Beforehand   Blanch tomatoes by plunging into boiling water for 15-20 seconds. (Length of time depends on ripeness of tomatoes.) Cool, remove skins, and core. To retain all juice, cut into small pieces on a plate. Mix seasonings.

Tray-Maid   Tomatoes, scallions, parsley, blended seasonings, broth, and chopped or powdered dill.

On Stage   Place tomatoes, onions, parsley, seasonings, and broth in blazer pan of chafing dish. Cover and simmer 20-25 minutes. Stir occasionally and press the tomatoes to the side and bottom of the pan to break them up and to distribute them evenly. Serve hot, sprinkled with dill. Makes 4 servings.

◄§ MENU ◊►

Fresh Tomato Bouillon
Cucumber Sandwiches
Deviled Ham-Chicken Sandwiches
Nutted Oatmeal Cookies
Hot Café-Cocoa

3.

The Meat
of the Meal

Here are some of the great chafing dish specialties—
around them scintillating dinners are built—Fondue Bourguignonne, Pork Chops Flamed in Applejack, Golden Ten-
derloins. This noble duty elevates your major-domo dish to
the summit of its handsome efficiency. Of course, you'll
receive all the plaudits and wisely take the bows.

JULIENNE OF BEEF ON CRUMPETS

4 ¼-inch thick slices rare roast
   beef
2 eggs
1 tablespoon Worcestershire
   sauce
½ teaspoon salt
¾ cup seasoned bread crumbs

4 tablespoons butter
1 10½-ounce can mushroom
   soup
¼ cup light cream
dash cayenne
hot buttered crumpets

Beforehand Cut beef into julienne strips. Beat eggs and add Worcestershire sauce and salt. Dip meat strips into egg mixture and then into bread crumbs. Have crumpets ready for the toaster.

Tray-Maid Beef strips, butter, soup, cream, cayenne, and crumpets.

On Stage Melt butter in blazer pan of chafing dish until it sizzles. Sauté meat strips, a few at a time, in butter until lightly browned (about 10 minutes). As you continue sautéing, it may be necessary to add more butter. As the meat gets done, remove it from the pan to a hot platter. Add soup and cream to pan juices, scraping up all brown bits from the bottom. Sprinkle a dash of cayenne. Add meat to the sauce, cover, and simmer 10 minutes, or until heated through. Serve on hot crumpets. Makes 4-6 servings.

✎§ MENU §✎

Julienne of Beef on Crumpets
Spinach Salad
Pears with Bel Paese Cheese
Coffee

BEEF STEAK MILANO

1½ pounds round steak
¼ cup salad oil
2 tablespoons wine vinegar
1 teaspoon salt
½ teaspoon freshly ground pepper

2 tablespoons butter
2 tablespoons chopped parsley
3 tablespoons dry red wine

Beforehand   Pound steak with edge of heavy plate or mallet until very thin. Mix oil, vinegar, salt, and pepper. Place meat in marinade, cover, and let stand at room temperature 2-3 hours. Just before starting to cook, remove meat from the marinade and drain lightly.

Tray-Maid   Marinated meat, butter, parsley, and wine.

On Stage   Heat butter in blazer pan of chafing dish until it sizzles. Place steak in pan and brown quickly on both sides. Remove steak to hot platter. Add parsley and wine to pan juices. Heat 1 minute, and pour over steak. Makes 4 servings.

◦§ MENU ?◦

Consommé with Avocado Garnish
Beef Steak Milano
Rice Pilaf
Wilted Lettuce and Cucumber Salad
Crème Brulée   Macaroons
Demitasse

FONDUE BOURGUIGNONNE

2 pounds lean tenderloin or filet of beef
½ pound butter
⅔ cup olive oil

Beforehand   Cut beef in ¾-inch cubes.

Tray-Maid   Beef cubes, butter, and oil.

On Stage   Over high heat bring butter and oil to sizzling in blazer pan of chafing dish. Provide each guest with a long fondue fork to spear a cube of meat and cook it to his taste in the sizzling hot butter and oil. The meat is then dipped in a choice of sauces. Makes 4 servings.

꽃 MENU 꽃

Fondue Bourguignonne
Béarnaise Sauce
Rémoulade Sauce
Curry Sauce
Chopped Parsley   } *add to suit*
Chopped Green Onion
Crisp French Bread
Fruit and Cheese
Coffee
Liqueurs

STEAK DIVINE

2 pounds sirloin steak
3 tablespoons sweet butter
2 tablespoons brandy
3 tablespoons sherry
1 teaspoon chopped chives

Beforehand Trim steak well and pound it with edge of heavy plate or mallet until flattened and thin. Cut into serving-size pieces. Warm the brandy before using.

Tray-Maid Steak, butter, brandy, sherry, and chives.

On Stage Melt butter in blazer pan of chafing dish until it sizzles. Brown steak on both sides in butter. Do not overcook. Pour brandy over meat and blaze. When flame dies out pour sherry over meat and sprinkle with chives. Heat 2 minutes longer, basting steak constantly with the sauce in the pan. Makes 4 servings.

◄§ MENU §►

Steak Divine
Stuffed Potato Boats
Broccoli Parmesan
Blackberry Pie
Coffee

STEAK RANCHERO

2 pounds ground top round steak	¼ teaspoon freshly ground pepper
2 eggs	⅛ teaspoon garlic powder
½ cup sour cream	1 large red onion
1 tablespoon chopped parsley	1 large green pepper
1 teaspoon salt	2 tablespoons salad oil

Beforehand Blend steak, eggs, sour cream, parsley, salt, pepper, and garlic powder. Let stand several hours, or overnight. Slice onion. Seed and dice green pepper. Just before starting to cook, form meat into a large cake one inch less in diameter than the blazer pan.

Tray-Maid Meat, oil, onion, and green pepper.

On Stage Heat oil in blazer pan of chafing dish until it sizzles. Using a large broad spatula, place meat in the pan. There should be a one-inch space between meat and edge of pan. Cover meat with onion and green pepper. Cook until browned on the bottom. Lower the heat and simmer 25-30 minutes. Baste occasionally with the juices as they collect in the pan. Just before serving, sprinkle with freshly ground pepper. Makes 4 servings.

⊷ MENU ⊶

Chinese Celery-Carrot-Raisin Salad
Steak Ranchero
Hot Fluffy Rice
Crumb-topped Baked Tomatoes
Apricot Cobbler
Coffee

FRANKFURTERS CALIFORNIAN

8 frankfurters (about 1 pound)	½ cup red California wine
1 tomato	2 tablespoons chili sauce
½ cup bouillon or consommé	2 teaspoons cornstarch
1 tablespoon minced onion	French bread or rolls

Beforehand Cut frankfurters into 1-inch diagonal slices. Peel and chop tomato. Combine frankfurters and tomato with bouillon, onion, wine, and chili sauce which has been mixed with cornstarch. Toast bread or rolls and keep them hot.

Tray-Maid Frankfurter mixture and bread.

On Stage Place all ingredients except bread in blazer pan of chafing dish. Cover and simmer 15-20 minutes, or until the mixture bubbles gently. Serve on French bread. Makes 4-6 servings.

⋞ MENU ⋟

Frankfurters Californian
Toasted French Bread
Crisp Vegetable Salad with Sour Cream Dressing
Frozen Lime Pie
Coffee

NOB HILL HAMBURGERS

2 pounds ground round steak	1 6-ounce can sliced mush-
¼ cup water	rooms
1 tablespoon chopped parsley	1 cup California burgundy
1 teaspoon salt	4 hamburger rolls
⅛ teaspoon pepper	butter
3 tablespoons butter	8 large sprigs watercress

Beforehand   Mix beef, water (this makes hamburger juicy), parsley, and seasonings. Form into 8 patties. Do not drain mushrooms. Split rolls, heat, and spread with butter. Have ready, washed, drained, crisp watercress.

Tray-Maid   Hamburgers, butter, mushrooms, wine, heated rolls, and watercress.

On Stage   Melt butter in blazer pan of chafing dish until it sizzles. Sauté hamburgers quickly on both sides to brown. Add mushrooms and wine. Simmer, uncovered, for 10 minutes. Baste several times while cooking. Just before serving, arrange the watercress on the hot rolls. Place a hamburger on each half of roll and spoon the sauce over it. Makes 4 servings.

⤷ MENU ⤶

Nob Hill Hamburgers
Pickle Relish Assortment
Baked Bean Casserole
Fresh Fruit and Cheese Tray
Coffee

CORNED BEEF MEXICALI

¼ cup butter
1 green pepper
1 tablespoon minced onion
¼ cup flour
½ teaspoon salt
1½ cups milk
1½ cups diced cooked corned beef

1 8½-ounce can whole kernel corn
4 egg yolks
½ cup light cream
1 tablespoon horseradish
2 20-ounce cans shoestring potatoes

Beforehand Seed and dice green pepper. Mix flour with salt. Beat egg yolks until thick, and gradually beat in cream and horseradish. Just before serving, heat the potatoes.

Tray-Maid Butter, green pepper, onion, seasoned flour, milk, corned beef, corn, egg-cream mixture, and potatoes.

On Stage Melt butter in blazer pan of chafing dish until it sizzles. Cook green pepper and onion in butter 5 minutes. Blend in seasoned flour. Gradually add milk, stirring until smooth. Cook, stirring constantly, until thickened. Add corned beef and corn. Slowly stir in egg-cream mixture. Cook over lowered heat until thick and smooth. Do not boil. Serve hot on shoestring potatoes. Makes 6-8 servings.

◄§ MENU §►

Corned Beef Mexicali
Tomato-Cabbage Slaw
Lime Ice
Iced or Hot Coffee

PERSIAN PLATTER

12 ounces mixed dried fruits
2 cups apricot nectar
2 cups water
¾ pound ground round steak
⅓ cup butter

2 10-ounce packages frozen
  chopped spinach
⅓ cup lemon juice
1 teaspoon salt
1⅓ cups rice

Beforehand Remove pits from fruits and cut them into large pieces. Cover with nectar and water and let stand several hours. Thaw and drain spinach. Just before starting, cook rice and keep it hot.

Tray-Maid Butter, meat, spinach, fruit, lemon juice, salt, and rice.

On Stage Heat butter in blazer pan of chafing dish until it sizzles. Sauté meat in butter until it loses redness. Add spinach and cook 5 minutes. Stir in marinated fruits and marinade, lemon juice, and salt. Blend well. Cover and simmer 25-30 minutes, or until the fruit is tender. If sauce is too thick, stir in enough hot water to produce desired consistency. Serve hot over hot rice. Makes 4 servings.

❧ MENU ❧

Persian Platter
Tossed Green Salad
Cheese and Crackers
Tea

HAM L'ORANGE

2 oranges	dash salt
2 lemons	dash pepper
¼ cup sugar	¼ cup chopped candied cherries
1½ cups water	
1½ cups port wine	4 ¼-inch thick slices boiled ham
½ cup apple jelly	
3 tablespoons vinegar	1 jigger brandy
1 tablespoon prepared mustard	

Beforehand Remove rind from oranges and lemons in very thin slivers. Reserve fruit for future use. Cut slices of ham in half. Just before starting to prepare the sauce, heat the brandy.

Tray-Maid Fruit rinds, sugar, water, wine, jelly, vinegar, mustard, salt, pepper, cherries, ham, and brandy.

On Stage Place fruit rinds, sugar, and water in blazer pan of chafing dish. Simmer, stirring occasionally to dissolve sugar, for 15 minutes. Remove rinds and add all remaining ingredients except brandy. Simmer 10 minutes longer, or until ham slices are heated through. Pour heated brandy over and blaze. Makes 6-8 servings.

✑ MENU ઙ∾

Cocktail Tomatoes
Ham L'Orange
Mashed Sweet Potatoes
Chinese Celery-Cabbage Salad
Petit Fours
Coffee   Tea

FLAMING HAM MANDARIN

4 ¼-inch thick slices boiled ham

2 tablespoons butter

1 12-ounce can mandarin orange sections

1 cup chicken bouillon

1 tablespoon cornstarch

1 tablespoon cold water

1 jigger Triple Sec

Beforehand Cut ham slices in two diagonally. Open, but do not drain, orange sections. Prepare chicken bouillon (this can be made by dissolving one chicken cube in one cup hot water). Blend cornstarch with the water until smooth.

Tray-Maid Ham, butter, orange sections, chicken bouillon, cornstarch paste, and Triple Sec.

On Stage Melt butter in blazer pan of chafing dish until it sizzles. Lightly brown the pieces of ham on both sides. Pour orange sections and bouillon over the ham. Cover and simmer 10 minutes. Place ham slices on a hot platter and keep them warm. Gradually stir cornstarch paste into the hot sauce, mixing until well blended. Cook, stirring constantly, until thick and clear. Return ham to sauce. Pour over Triple Sec and blaze. Serve as soon as the flame disappears. Makes 4 servings.

⊸§ MENU §⊸

Mushroom Consommé
Flaming Ham Mandarin
Rice
Green Salad
Almond Cakes
Jasmine Tea in Covered Cups

KIDNEY À LA REINE

18 lamb kidneys	½ teaspoon salt
4 cups beef consommé	gravy seasoning
1 tablespoon salad oil	1 tablespoon chopped parsley
2 tablespoons butter	¼ cup sherry
1¼ tablespoons flour	toast points

Beforehand   Remove membrane and connective tissue from kidneys and cut in half. Boil consommé until it is reduced to 3 cups. Mix flour and salt. Just before starting, make toast points.

Tray-Maid   Oil, butter, kidneys, seasoned flour, consommé, gravy seasoning, parsley, sherry, and toast points.

On Stage   Heat oil and butter in blazer pan of chafing dish until they sizzle. Cook kidneys in oil and butter until lightly browned (about 10 minutes). Sprinkle flour over kidneys and stir until well blended into the fat in the pan. Gradually stir in the consommé, mixing until the sauce is smooth. Cook, stirring constantly, until thickened. Add a few drops of gravy seasoning to get the desired brown color. Stir in parsley and wine and heat to a simmer. Serve hot over toast points. Makes 4-6 servings.

⋙ MENU ⋘

Artichoke Hearts Vinaigrette
Kidneys à la Reine
Stuffed Mushrooms
Macédoine of Fresh Fruit
Coffee

BORIS' SPECIAL KIDNEY DISH

4 veal kidneys	4 slices bacon
or	1 cup plain yogurt
8 lamb kidneys	1 tablespoon chopped parsley
¼ cup flour	1 tablespoon finely minced
1 teaspoon salt	onion
⅛ teaspoon pepper	2 cups hot cooked brown rice

Beforehand   Remove membrane and connective tissue from kidneys. Wash, drain well, and cut into thin slices. Mix flour, salt, and pepper. Dredge kidney slices in flour. Cut bacon into snippets. Just before starting, begin cooking the rice so that it will be ready for serving.

Tray-Maid   Bacon snippets, sliced kidneys, yogurt, parsley, onion, and hot rice.

On Stage   Sauté bacon in blazer pan of chafing dish until crisp and browned. Remove bacon from pan and keep it hot. Sauté kidneys in bacon fat until browned (about 8-10 minutes). Pour yogurt over kidneys. Add parsley and onion. Stir gently with a fork to blend. Cover and simmer 2-3 minutes. Serve, sprinkled with bacon, on hot rice. Makes 4 servings.

◄§   MENU   §►

Broiled Dates Wrapped in Bacon
Boris' Special Kidney Dish
Asparagus with Lemon-Butter Sauce
Cheese Cake
Coffee

LEMONY LAMB BALLS

1½ pounds lean ground lamb	½ teaspoon salt
½ cup finely chopped green onion	2 teaspoons grated lemon rind
½ cup finely chopped parsley	3 eggs
¾ cup long-grain rice	½ cup lemon juice
1 teaspoon sage	6 cups beef consommé
1 teaspoon celery salt	French bread

Beforehand Mix lamb, onion, parsley, rice, seasonings, lemon rind, and 1 egg. Form mixture into 1-inch balls.

Tray-Maid Lamb balls, consommé, eggs, lemon juice, and French bread.

On Stage Place consommé in blazer pan of chafing dish over high heat and bring it to a boil. Drop balls into consommé. Cover and simmer 25-30 minutes, or until rice is tender. (Some of rice will pop out of the balls.) Beat the remaining 2 eggs with the lemon juice until well blended. Add about 1 cup of hot consommé to egg mixture, beating constantly until creamy. Quickly stir into remaining consommé, mixing briskly until well blended. Serve hot with chunks of French bread to dunk up the sauce. Makes 4-6 servings.

⋙ MENU ⋘

Fresh Sliced Mushrooms Vinaigrette
Lemony Lamb Balls
Braised Celery
Banana Cream Pie
Coffee

LAMB WITH RHINE WINE

¼ cup butter
¼ pound mushrooms *or* 1 3-ounce can sliced broiled-in-butter mushrooms
¼ cup diced green pepper
¼ cup flour
1 teaspoon salt
⅛ teaspoon freshly ground pepper

½ cup light cream
1 cup bouillon
2 cups diced cooked lamb
2 tablespoons sliced stuffed olives
¼ teaspoon marjoram
½ cup rhine wine
hot buttered noodles

Beforehand   Slice mushrooms or drain canned mushrooms. Mix flour with salt and pepper. Mix cream with bouillon. Just before starting, prepare noodles and keep them hot.

Tray-Maid   Butter, mushrooms, green pepper, seasoned flour, cream and bouillon mixture, lamb, olives, marjoram, wine, and hot buttered noodles.

On Stage   Melt butter in the blazer pan of chafing dish until it sizzles. Add mushrooms and green pepper. Cook, stirring occasionally, for about 10 minutes, or until mushrooms are light brown. Sprinkle with seasoned flour, stir, and mix. Add cream mixture. Cook, stirring constantly, until thickened. Add lamb, olives, marjoram, and wine. Cover and simmer 5 minutes longer, or until heated through. Serve on hot buttered noodles. Makes 4-6 servings.

◄§ MENU ‎§►

Lamb with Rhine Wine
Hot Buttered Noodles
Asparagus Tips
Macaroon Pudding
Coffee

MARIO'S CURRY OF LAMB

2 cups diced cooked lamb
2 tablespoons butter or margarine
2 tablespoons chopped green onion
1 tablespoon flour
1-2 teaspoons curry powder (to taste)
¼ teaspoon grated lemon rind
1 10½-ounce can condensed consommé
¾ cup water
salt and pepper (to taste)
1 egg yolk
1 tablespoon lemon juice
grated coconut

Beforehand   Combine flour, curry powder, and lemon rind. Blend consommé with water. Beat egg yolk until lemony.

Tray-Maid   Lamb, butter, green onion, flour mixture, consommé, salt, pepper, egg yolk, lemon juice, and grated coconut.

On Stage   Heat butter in blazer pan of chafing dish until it sizzles. Sauté onion in butter until it is golden brown. Stir in flour mixture. Gradually blend in consommé and stir with a wooden spoon until the sauce is smooth and creamy. Add lamb, and salt and pepper to taste. Cover and simmer for 10 minutes. Reduce heat to minimum and blend in egg yolk and lemon juice. Serve immediately with a sprinkling of grated coconut. Makes 4 servings.

◄§   MENU   §►

Avocado-Orange Cup
Mario's Curry of Lamb
Hot Fluffy Rice
Chutney
Green salad
Pistachio Ice Cream   Macaroons
Beer   Coffee

MINTED LAMB PATTIES

1½ pounds ground lean lamb
2 tablespoons chopped fresh mint *or* dried mint
1 teaspoon salt
⅛ teaspoon freshly ground pepper

2 eggs
½ cup sour cream
3 tablespoons butter
3 tablespoons white wine
⅓ cup sesame seeds

Beforehand   Mix lamb, mint, salt, pepper, eggs, and sour cream. Shape mixture into 8 patties.

Tray-Maid   Lamb patties, butter, wine, and sesame seeds.

On Stage   Melt butter in blazer pan of chafing dish until it sizzles. Lower heat slightly and gently cook the patties (about 10 minutes on each side). When the patties are lightly browned, pour the wine over and simmer 3 minutes. Serve hot, sprinkled with sesame seeds. Makes 4 servings.

◄§   MENU   §►

Minted Lamb Patties
Baked Stuffed Potatoes
Russian Vegetable Salad
Blueberry Tarts
Demitasse

LAMB CHOPS À LA TANGERINE

8 ¾-inch thick loin lamb chops
2 tablespoons sliced green onion
3 tangerines
¼ cup dry white wine
¾ cup tangerine juice

⅓ cup lemon juice
⅓ cup light brown sugar
1 tablespoon grated lemon rind
1 teaspoon salt
⅛ teaspoon pepper

Beforehand Trim excess fat from chops and set it aside. Peel tangerines, removing the thin strings, and separate them into sections. Cut the sections in half and remove the seeds. Mix lemon juice and tangerine juice and stir in sugar and grated rind. Mix salt and pepper.

Tray-Maid Chops, trimmed fat, green onions, tangerines, wine, blended juices, salt, and pepper.

On Stage Melt lamb fat in blazer pan of chafing dish until it sizzles. Brown chops on both sides (about 8 minutes for each side). Remove to hot platter. Spoon out all but 2 tablespoons of the remaining fat. Sauté onions and tangerines in fat until tangerines are slightly glazed. Arrange chops over the fruit in the pan. Pour wine and juice mixture over. Sprinkle with salt and pepper. Cover and simmer 10-15 minutes, basting occasionally, until tender. Makes 4 servings.

◄§ MENU ɓ►

Olives, Radishes, Dill Beans
Lamb Chops à la Tangerine
Rice
Marrons Glacés
Coffee

PO VALLEY LAMB CHOPS

4 ¾-inch thick lamb shoulder
  chops
1 medium onion
2 medium zucchini squash
1 tablespoon salad oil
1½ teaspoons seasoned salt

⅛ teaspoon pepper
4 thick slices tomato
½ teaspoon oregano
dash salt
dash pepper

Beforehand Trim excess fat from chops and set it aside. Flatten chops slightly by pounding with edge of heavy plate or mallet. Slice onion. Wash zucchini and cut it into 1-inch slices. Mix seasoned salt and pepper. Sprinkle tomato slices with oregano, salt, and pepper.

Tray-Maid Chops, onion, zucchini, salad oil, mixed seasonings, and seasoned tomato slices.

On Stage Melt lamb fat in blazer pan of chafing dish until it sizzles. Brown chops and onions in the fat until onions are golden brown. Remove chops from the pan and keep them hot. Add salad oil to fat in the pan. Cook zucchini, sprinkling with mixed seasonings and turning often, until just lightly browned. When all zucchini is browned, spread it evenly in the pan. Cover with chops and top with tomato slices. Cover and simmer 25-30 minutes, or until chops are tender. Makes 4 servings.

◄§ MENU §►

Po Valley Lamb Chops
Potatoes Au Gratin
Mixed Fresh Fruit Compote
Coffee

FLAMING LIVER SLIVERS

1½ pound calf's liver
1 cup French dressing
1 tablespoon dry white wine
¾ cup flour
½ teaspoon salt

¼ teaspoon freshly ground pepper
3 tablespoons butter
1 jigger cognac
4 cups hot buttered rice

Beforehand Cut liver into thin slivers. Dip slices into French dressing mixed with wine and let stand at room temperature for 1 hour. Then dredge slices with flour mixed with seasonings. Just before starting, heat cognac and prepare rice.

Tray-Maid Liver, butter, cognac, and rice.

On Stage Melt butter in blazer pan of chafing dish until it sizzles. Sauté liver quickly on both sides until lightly browned. Do not overcook. Pour cognac over and blaze. Serve liver on rice as soon as the flame dies out. Makes 4-6 servings.

◄§ MENU §►

Celery and Carrot Curls
Flaming Liver Slivers
Hot Buttered Rice
Frenched Green Beans
Peaches Poached in Burgundy Wine
Coffee

CALF'S LIVER IN RED WINE

1½ pounds calf's liver
3 tablespoons flour
1 teaspoon salt
½ teaspoon freshly ground pepper

1 teaspoon powdered sage
3 tablespoons olive oil
¼ cup dry red wine
toast points

Beforehand Cut liver into very thin slices (or have the butcher do it for you). Blend flour with seasonings. Dredge liver slices in seasoned flour. Just before starting make toast points.

Tray-Maid Floured liver, oil, wine, and toast points.

On Stage Heat oil in blazer pan of chafing dish until it sizzles. Sauté liver in oil quickly, (about 3 minutes on each side). Add wine and simmer 2 minutes. Serve on toast points.

⊸ MENU ⊱

Cheese Puffs
Calf's Liver in Red Wine
Toast Points
Green Beans Almandine
Cherry Ice Cream with Cherry Brandy
Coffee

PACIFIC ISLE DINNER

1½ cups sliced green celery
2 cups cubed cooked roast pork
2 teaspoons soy sauce
1 teaspoon salt
1 tablespoon curry powder
2 tablespoons butter
2 medium onions
1 green pepper

1 cup currants or raisins
1 cup beef bouillon
½ cup salted peanuts
1 4-ounce can pimientos
1½ tablespoons cornstarch
1 tablespoon water
hot buttered rice

Beforehand Cook celery in salted water until just tender, and drain. Mix celery, pork, soy sauce, salt, and curry powder, stirring occasionally to blend flavors. Slice onions, seeded green pepper, and pimientos. Blend cornstarch and water. Just before starting, prepare the rice and keep it hot.

Tray-Maid Seasoned celery-pork, butter, onions, green pepper, currants, bouillon, peanuts, pimiento, cornstarch paste, and hot rice.

On Stage Melt butter in blazer pan of chafing dish until it sizzles. Sauté onion and green pepper in butter for 5 minutes. Add seasoned celery-pork mixture, currants, and bouillon. Cover and simmer 15 minutes. Add nuts and pimiento and simmer 5 minutes longer. Stir in cornstarch paste and gently mix with a fork. Cook until the mixture is slightly thickened and the sauce is clear. Serve on hot rice. Makes 4-6 servings.

◄§ MENU ᵺ►

Pacific Isle Dinner
Hot Rolls   Radish Roses
Frozen Orange Whip
Cookies   Demitasse

GOLDEN PORK TENDERLOIN

2 pounds smoked pork tenderloin
1 cup apple cider
¼ cup orange juice

¼ cup dry sherry
1 clove garlic, minced
1 tablespoon soy sauce
2 tablespoons butter

Beforehand Cut uncooked tenderized tenderloin into 8 slices. Pound pieces with mallet or rim of heavy plate to flatten. Mix cider, orange juice, sherry, garlic, and soy sauce, and pour over the pieces of tenderloin. Marinate 3-4 hours, or overnight.

Tray-Maid Tenderloin in marinade and butter.

On stage Melt butter in blazer pan of chafing dish until it sizzles. Remove pieces of tenderloin from marinade, drain slightly, and sauté in butter over lowered heat (about 10 minutes on each side). Pour marinade over the meat. Cover and simmer 10 minutes longer. Serve hot. Makes 4-6 servings.

⋙ MENU ⋘

Vichyssoise
Golden Pork Tenderloin
Green Noodles
Cauliflower Vinaigrette
Strawberries in White Wine
Coffee

FLAMING BAVARIAN PORK CHOPS

6 ¾-inch thick smoked loin pork chops
½ teaspoon seasoned salt
¼ teaspoon seasoned pepper
¾ cup tart applesauce
1 cup beef bouillon
⅓ cup applejack

Beforehand   Trim excess fat from chops and save it. Sprinkle chops with seasoned salt and pepper. Mix applesauce with bouillon.

Tray-Maid   Trimmed fat, seasoned chops, applesauce mixture, and applejack.

On Stage   Heat trimmed fat in blazer pan of chafing dish until it sizzles. Place chops in fat and cook for 5 minutes on both sides. Add applesauce mixture. Cover and simmer 30 minutes, or until chops are tender. Remove cover and cook until the pan juices are reduced by half. Pour applejack over and flame. Serve as soon as the flame is out. Makes 6 servings.

◄§   MENU   §►

Sauerkraut-Tomato Juice
Flaming Bavarian Pork Chops
Potato Puff
Tossed Green Salad
Fruit   Cheese
Wine   Coffee

TEXAS TOPPERS

¾ pound ground round steak
¾ pound sausage meat
1 teaspoon monosodium gluta-
    mate
1 teaspoon garlic salt
⅛ teaspoon pepper
1-2 teaspoons chili powder
2 tablespoons butter

½ cup finely sliced celery
¼ cup finely chopped onion
1 pound fresh tomatoes
1 8-ounce can tomato sauce
¼ cup sliced ripe olives
large corn chips
shredded lettuce

Beforehand   Mix meats with seasonings by tossing lightly with a fork. Peel and dice tomatoes on a plate to save the juice. Just before serving, heat corn chips and shred lettuce.

Tray-Maid   Butter, celery, onion, seasoned meat, tomatoes, tomato sauce, olives, corn chips, and lettuce.

On Stage   Melt butter in blazer pan of large chafing dish until it sizzles. Sauté celery and onion in butter until lightly browned (about 10 minutes). Add meat and cook, stirring with a fork, until it loses redness and is crumbly. Add tomatoes and sauce. Simmer 35-40 minutes, or until quite thick. Just before serving, stir in olives. Serve hot on corn chips and top with lettuce. Makes 6-8 servings.

⊷ MENU ⊶

Vegetable Stick Tray
Texas Toppers
Applesauce Cookies
Iced Coffee with Ice Cream Float

CHINESE SAUSAGE CAKES

2 large green peppers
2½ pounds sausage meat
1 egg
½ cup fine saltine cracker crumbs
½ teaspoon seasoned pepper
¼ cup salad oil
2½ cups chicken bouillon
1 8-ounce can shredded pineapple

2 tablespoons diced candied ginger
6 tablespoons cornstarch
⅔ cup vinegar
1 cup light corn syrup
4 teaspoons soy sauce
1 cup dry sherry

Beforehand   Wash, seed, and cut green peppers into 1-inch pieces. Mix sausage meat, egg, cracker crumbs, and seasoned pepper and form mixture into 16 flat cakes. Mix cornstarch with vinegar and syrup until smooth.

Tray-Maid   Sausage cakes, oil, bouillon, green pepper, pineapple, cornstarch mixture, sherry, soy sauce and ginger.

On Stage   Heat oil in blazer pan of chafing dish until it sizzles. Sauté cakes in oil, a few at a time, until browned on both sides and done (about 25 minutes). Remove cakes from pan and keep them hot. Drain off excess fat but let all the brown specks remain in the pan. Add 1 cup of bouillon, pineapple, and green pepper. Cover and simmer 10 minutes. Add remaining bouillon and cornstarch mixture. Cook, stirring constantly, until thick and clear. Stir in sherry, soy sauce, and ginger. Arrange cakes in the pan and spoon the sauce over them. Cover and simmer 10 minutes longer. Makes 8 servings.

SWEETBREADS AND PEAS IN CELERY TOAST BASKETS

1 pair sweetbreads	2 tablespoons flour
1¼ cups water	1 teaspoon seasoned salt
1¼ cups sauterne	2 tablespoons sour cream
½ teaspoon salt	1 cup cooked peas
1 bay leaf	hot toast baskets*
3 whole cloves	paprika
2 tablespoons butter	

Beforehand   Soak sweetbreads in cold water for 20 minutes. Mix water, sauterne, plain salt, bay leaf, and cloves and bring to a boil. Plunge sweetbreads into boiling water and simmer for 30 minutes. Drain sweetbreads, reserving the stock, and place them in cold water. When cool, remove fat, gristle, and membrane and break them (do not cut) into small pieces. Mix flour with seasoned salt. Make toast baskets.

Tray-Maid   Butter, seasoned flour, reserved stock, sour cream, peas, sweetbreads, toast baskets, and paprika.

On Stage   Melt butter in blazer pan of chafing dish until it sizzles. Blend in seasoned flour. Add reserved stock and mix until smooth. Cook, stirring constantly, until thickened. Add cream, peas, and sweetbreads. Heat just to simmering. Serve hot in baskets and sprinkle with paprika. Makes 4-6 servings.

* Remove crusts from 4-6 slices of fresh bread. Spread with softened butter and sprinkle with celery salt. Fit each slice in medium-size buttered muffin tin. Toast in hot oven (400°) 5-8 minutes, or until lightly browned.

TANGY TONGUE ON PINEAPPLE SLICES

1¼ pounds cooked smoked tongue
2 tablespoons flour
1 teaspoon prepared mustard
⅓ cup firmly packed light brown sugar

1 12-ounce can apricot nectar
¼ cup lemon juice
⅓ cup dried currants
4 slices pineapple

Beforehand Cut tongue into 12 slices. Blend flour with mustard and add sugar and lemon juice, mixing well. Add nectar and currants.

Tray-Maid Sliced tongue, nectar mixture, and pineapple slices.

On Stage Place nectar mixture in blazer pan of chafing dish. Cook, stirring constantly, until thickened. Simmer 5 minutes. Arrange pineapple slices in sauce and place 3 slices of tongue on each piece of pineapple. Baste with the sauce. Simmer 10 minutes longer, or until pineapple and tongue are heated through. Makes 4 servings.

◄§ MENU §►

Eggs à la Russe
Tangy Tongue on Pineapple Slices
Baked Squares of Winter Squash
Onion-seasoned Matzos
Old Fashioned Custard
Coffee

MUSTARD VEAL CHOPS IN OLIVE SAUCE

4 veal chops with kidneys
3 tablespoons butter
2 tablespoons flour
1 teaspoon salt
dash freshly ground pepper

2 teaspoons dry English mustard
1½ cups light cream
½ cup sliced stuffed olives
1 tablespoon olive liquid

Beforehand   Wipe chops and sprinkle with salt and pepper. Mix flour, salt, pepper, and mustard. Add olive liquid to olives.

Tray-Maid   Chops, butter, seasoned flour, cream, and olives.

On Stage   Melt butter in blazer pan of chafing dish until it sizzles. Brown chops in butter until evenly browned. Cover and simmer, turning occasionally, until tender (about 45 minutes). Remove chops to a hot platter. Blend seasoned flour into the liquid in the pan, mixing until smooth. Gradually stir in cream until the mixture is smooth. Cook, stirring constantly, until thickened. Stir in olives and heat 3 minutes longer. Pour sauce over chops. Makes 4 servings.

◄§   MENU   ε►

Mustard Veal Chops in Olive Sauce
Buttered Hot Rice
Baked Tomatoes
Hearts of Celery
Raspberry Sherbert   Coffee

HUNGARIAN VEAL CHOPS

4 1-inch thick loin veal chops
with kidneys
1 cup yogurt
1 teaspoon dill

1 teaspoon paprika
1 teaspoon seasoned salt
½ teaspoon pepper
¼ cup finely sliced onion

Beforehand Trim excess fat from chops and set it aside. Blend yogurt with seasonings and pour it over the chops. Let stand at room temperature for 2-3 hours. Just before starting, remove chops from marinade and dry well. Reserve the marinade.

Tray-Maid Fat trimmings, chops, onions, and yogurt marinade.

On Stage Heat pieces of fat in blazer pan of chafing dish until they sizzle. Sauté onions in fat until lightly browned. Push onions to one side and sauté chops in fat until browned on both sides. If there is not enough fat, add 1 tablespoon butter. Pour marinade over chops. Cover and simmer 30 minutes, or until the meat is tender. Serve with the sauce left in the pan. Makes 4 servings.

◄§ MENU §►

Hungarian Veal Chops
Green Beans   Savory Potatoes
Peach Melba
Demitasse with Lemon Rind

SWISS VEAL ROLLS

2 pounds veal cutlet, cut very thin
6 slices boiled ham
¾ cup coarsely shredded imported swiss cheese
freshly ground pepper
½ cup butter
½ cup dry white wine
chopped parsley

Beforehand   Cut veal into 12 pieces. Cut ham slices in half diagonally. Place a slice of ham on a slice of veal and sprinkle with cheese and pepper. Roll and tie with heavy thread or secure with wooden picks or small skewers.

Tray-Maid   Veal rolls, butter, wine, and parsley.

On Stage   Melt butter in blazer pan of chafing dish until it sizzles. Brown veal rolls in butter, turning to brown all sides evenly. Pour wine over the rolls. Cover and simmer 20-25 minutes, or until meat is tender. Sprinkle with parsley. Makes 6 servings.

◄§   MENU   §►

Cold Tomato Bisque
Swiss Veal Rolls
Maître d'Hôtel Onions
Mincemeat Pie
Coffee

AMALFI VEAL SCALLOPS

1½ pounds veal, sliced thin
¼ cup flour
1 teaspoon salt
⅛ teaspoon freshly ground pepper
3 tablespoons butter

1 cup beef bouillon
1 5-ounce can deviled ham
¼ cup dry vermouth
chopped parsley
hot buttered noodles

Beforehand Cut veal into serving-size pieces. Pound pieces with edge of heavy plate or mallet until they are paper thin. Mix flour with salt and pepper. Dredge veal in seasoned flour until well coated. Just before starting, prepare noodles and keep them hot.

Tray-Maid Butter, floured veal, bouillon, ham, vermouth, parsley, and noodles.

On Stage Melt butter in blazer pan of chafing dish until it sizzles. Sauté veal scallops in butter until lightly browned and tender (about 15 minutes). Place them on a hot platter. Stir bouillon into the pan juices. Add ham, a tablespoon at a time, blending well after each addition. When mixture is smooth, cover and simmer 5 minutes. Remove cover and stir in vermouth. Place veal in the sauce. Simmer 5 minutes longer, or until heated through. Sprinkle with parsley. Serve on noodles. Makes 6 servings.

◄§ MENU §►

Amalfi Veal Scallops
Buttered Noodles
Grapefruit-Avocado Salad
Éclairs Filled with Ice Cream
Coffee   Cordials

4.

A Chafing Dish is Good for Birds

"A chicken in every chafing dish" must have been the true sentiment of the philosophical Roi, Louis XIV. This more distinguished statement would then have echoed through the valleys and peaks of prosperity ever after. For what is more beguiling fare than a sweet bird cooked in sauce, an art calling for the chef's most practical, yet most delicate art.

CHICKEN ÉLÉGANT

¼ cup chopped onion	1 2½-ounce can mushrooms
3 tablespoons butter	2 cups cubed cooked chicken
3 tablespoons flour	1 medium avocado
1 tablespoon salt	1 tablespoon lemon juice
½ teaspoon crushed tarragon	6 patty shells
2 cups light cream	paprika
1 cup grated American cheese	

Beforehand Mix flour with salt and tarragon. Drain mushrooms. Peel and remove seed from avocado. Cut it into cubes and sprinkle with lemon juice to prevent darkening. Heat patty shells.

Tray-Maid Onion, butter, seasoned flour, cream, cheese, mushrooms, chicken, avocado, patty shells, and paprika.

On Stage Melt butter in blazer pan of chafing dish until it sizzles. Sauté onion in butter until soft. Stir in seasoned flour. Blend in cream and mix until smooth. Cook, stirring constantly, until sauce is thickened. Add cheese and stir until it melts. Add mushrooms, chicken, and avocado. Cover and simmer 15 minutes, or until heated through. Serve hot in patty shells. Garnish with dash of paprika. Makes 4-6 servings.

◄§ MENU §►

Tossed Greens and Grapefruit Salad
Chicken Élégant
Deep-Dish Peach Pie
Iced Minted Tea

TURKISH CHICKEN RAGOUT

2 cups diced cooked chicken
3 tablespoons butter
2 tablespoons thinly sliced green onion
1 cup long-grain rice

2 10½-ounce cans beef consommé
½ cup water
1 large tomato
toasted almonds

Beforehand   Peel and dice tomato.

Tray-Maid   Chicken, butter, green onions, rice, consommé, water, tomato, and almonds.

On Stage   Melt butter in blazer pan of chafing dish until it sizzles. Sauté chicken and onion in butter for 5 minutes. Remove from pan. Sprinkle rice into the fat remaining in the pan. Stir and cook until the rice is slightly yellow in color. Add chicken and all remaining ingredients except nuts. Mix well. Cover and simmer, stirring occasionally, 25-30 minutes, or until rice is just tender. Serve hot sprinkled with almonds. Makes 4-6 servings.

✌ MENU ✍

Iced Vegetable Juice Cocktail
Turkish Chicken Ragout
Apple-Chinese Cabbage Slaw
Mocha Layer Cake
Coffee

CHICKEN AND HAM À LA CRÈME

1 tablespoon butter
1 tablespoon flour
½ teaspoon salt
⅛ teaspoon freshly ground pepper
1 6-ounce can button mushrooms

¾ cup heavy cream
1 cup diced cooked chicken
1 cup diced cooked ham
2 tablespoons chopped parsley
4-6 patty shells

Beforehand Mix flour, salt, and pepper. Do not drain mushrooms. Heat patty shells.

Tray-Maid Butter, seasoned flour, mushrooms, cream, chicken, ham, parsley, and patty shells.

On Stage Melt butter in blazer pan of chafing dish until it sizzles. Blend in seasoned flour until smooth. Gradually stir in mushroom liquid and cream, mixing until well blended. Cook, stirring constantly until thickened (about 10 minutes). Add mushrooms, chicken, ham, and parsley. Simmer 5 minutes longer. Serve hot in patty shells. Makes 4-6 servings.

◦§ MENU §◦

Half Grapefruit
Chicken and Ham à la Crème
Tomato-Artichoke Heart Salad
Coffee Mousse
Demitasse   Liqueur

CHICKEN BREASTS DOMENIQUE

2 whole chicken breasts	½ cup brandy
½ teaspoon salt	½ cup sliced black olives
⅛ teaspoon white pepper	¼ cup heavy cream
2 tablespoons butter	toasted slivered almonds
2 tablespoons salad oil	
2 tablespoons sliced green onion	

Beforehand   Split breasts to make 4 pieces and carefully remove skin and bones. Flatten slightly with edge of heavy plate or mallet and sprinkle with salt and pepper.

Tray-Maid   Chicken breasts, butter, oil, onion, brandy, olives, cream, and almonds.

On Stage   Heat butter and oil in blazer pan of chafing dish until sizzling. Place chicken breasts and onion in the pan. Sauté until browned on both sides (about 20 to 25 minutes). Add brandy. Cover and simmer 20-25 minutes longer, or until tender. Add olives and cream. Heat 5 minutes longer. Just before serving, sprinkle with almonds. Makes 4 servings.

◄§ MENU §►

Black Bean Soup Cup
Chicken Breasts Domenique
Green Noodles
Orange Sherbert
Coffee

DEVILED CHICKEN LEGS

8 plump chicken legs	4 tablespoons butter
½ cup flour	¾ cup chili sauce
1 teaspoon salt	¼ cup water
1 teaspoon chili powder	dash Tabasco sauce
¼ teaspoon pepper	

Beforehand Wash and dry chicken legs. Mix flour with seasonings. Toss legs with seasoned flour in a paper bag. Mix chili sauce, water, and Tabasco sauce.

Tray-Maid Floured chicken legs, butter, and chili-sauce mixture.

On Stage Melt butter in blazer pan of chafing dish until it sizzles. Brown floured chicken legs in butter, turning often. Pour over chili-sauce mixture, cover, and simmer, turning legs occasionally, until they are tender (about 25-30 minutes). Makes 4 servings.

⋖ৡ MENU ৡ⋗

Deviled Chicken Legs
Rice Pilaf
Marinated Zucchini Salad
Chocolate Soufflé
Coffee

CHICKEN LIVERS IN CREAM

1 pound chicken livers	1 jigger brandy
salt	1 cup cream
freshly ground pepper	chopped parsley
¼ cup butter	4 slices French toast
1 tablespoon minced green onion	sesame seeds

Beforehand Wash livers and drain them well. Cut them in half and sprinkle them with salt and pepper. Sprinkle French toast with sesame seeds and keep it hot.

Tray-Maid Livers, butter, onion, brandy, cream, parsley, and French toast.

On Stage Melt butter in blazer pan of chafing dish until it sizzles. Sauté livers and onion in butter until lightly browned. Pour brandy over and blaze. When the flame dies out, stir in cream. Cook, stirring constantly, until the sauce is slightly thickened. Sprinkle with parsley and serve hot on French toast. Makes 4 servings.

✦§ MENU ᐂ✦

Chicken Livers in Cream
French Toast
Molded Avocado and Orange Salad on Watercress
French-style Cookies
Coffee

QUICK AND SAVORY CHICKEN À LA KING

3 packages frozen chicken à la
   king
¼ teaspoon powdered rosemary
1 cup cooked peas

3 tablespoons sherry
¼ cup heavy cream
paprika
6 patty shells

Beforehand Thaw frozen chicken à la king. Chill cream and whip it just before starting.

Tray-Maid Chicken à la king, rosemary, peas, sherry, whipped cream, paprika, and patty shells.

On Stage Place chicken à la king, rosemary, and peas in blazer pan of chafing dish over low heat. Heat, stirring occasionally, until gently simmering and heated through. Stir in sherry and heat 3 minutes longer. Just before serving, fold in whipped cream. Serve in patty shells sprinkled with paprika. Makes 6 servings.

◄§ PATIO MENU §►

Chilled Tomato Soup with Basil
Quick and Savory Chicken à la King
Romaine-Crumpled Bacon Salad
Double Ice Cream Cones
Iced Coffee

DUCKLING SAUTERNE ON GREEN RICE

3 cups cubed cooked duckling
1 teaspoon salt
⅛ teaspoon freshly ground pepper
6 tablespoons butter
1 pound fresh mushrooms

2 10½-ounce cans cream of celery soup
½ cup light cream
1½ cups cooked peas
½ cup sauterne
green rice*

Beforehand Sprinkle duck with salt and pepper. Slice mushrooms. Just before starting, prepare green rice and keep it hot.

Tray-Maid Duckling, butter, mushrooms, soup, cream, peas, wine, and green rice.

On Stage Melt butter in blazer pan of chafing dish until it sizzles. Sauté mushrooms in butter until tender and golden brown. Stir in soup and cream. Blend carefully. Cover and simmer 20-25 minutes. Stir in peas and wine. Simmer 10 minutes longer. Serve hot on green rice. Makes 6-8 servings.

◄§ MENU §►

Orange-Avocado Cup
Duckling Sauterne on Green Rice
Vanilla Chiffon Roll
Spiced Tea

* Add ½ cup chopped parsley and ¼ cup finely cut chives to 4 cups hot buttered rice.

DUCK IN CREAM

1 4-5 pound duckling	1 teaspoon paprika
1 bay leaf	½ teaspoon poultry seasoning
8 peppercorns	2 tablespoons sliced green
1 teaspoon salt	onion
1 medium carrot	4 tablespoons butter
3 sprigs parsley	1 6-ounce can broiled mush-
water	rooms
½ cup flour	1 cup light cream
1 teaspoon salt	

Beforehand Wash and cut duckling into serving-size pieces and place in saucepan with bay leaf, peppercorns, 1 teaspoon salt, carrot cut into pieces, and parsley. Add water just to cover and simmer, covered, about 1 hour, or until just tender. Do not overcook. Drain, reserving stock. Mix flour, 1 teaspoon salt, paprika, and poultry seasoning. Dredge pieces of duckling in seasoned flour. Do not drain mushrooms.

Tray-Maid Floured pieces of duckling, butter, green onion, mushrooms, duck stock, and cream.

On Stage Melt butter in blazer pan of chafing dish until it sizzles. Sauté duck in butter until lightly browned on all sides. Add onion, mushrooms, and 1 cup of duck stock. Cover and simmer 15 minutes. Pour cream over and simmer 10 minutes longer. Makes 6 servings.

✿§ MENU ℘

Celery and Olive Tray

Duck in Cream

Mashed Potatoes   Green Beans Amandine

Plum Pudding   Coffee

DUCK-A-TASH

1 package frozen succotash
   or
1½ cups fresh succotash
2 cups cubed cooked duck
2 10½-ounce cans condensed
   cheddar cheese soup

2 tablespoons diced pimiento
¼ cup light cream
¼ cup sherry
toast points

Beforehand Cook frozen or fresh succotash and drain well. Prepare toast points just before starting.

Tray-Maid Soup, cream, duck, succotash, pimiento, sherry, and toast points.

On Stage Blend soup and cream in blazer pan of chafing dish until smooth. Heat, stirring occasionally, until gently simmering (about 8-10 minutes). Add succotash, duck, and pimiento. Cover and simmer 10 minutes longer, or until piping hot. Just before serving stir in sherry. Serve on toast points. Makes 6 servings.

◦§ BRUNCH MENU §◦

Frisky Sours
Duck-a-Tash
Small Danish Sweet Buns
Coffee

ROCK CORNISH HENS WITH BLAZING WINE SAUCE

6 Rock Cornish hens
3 tablespoons butter
¾ cup red currant jelly
2 tablespoons lemon juice
½ cup water
1 teaspoon salt

dash freshly ground pepper
⅛ teaspoon ground cloves
¾ cup port wine
3 tablespoons pan liquid from roasted hens
3 tablespoons brandy

Beforehand Roast hens according to package directions. While hens are roasting, mix butter, jelly, lemon juice, water, salt, pepper, and cloves. When hens are done, remove from pan and keep hot on hot platter. Measure pan liquid. Heat brandy just before starting.

Tray-Maid Jelly mixture, wine, pan liquid, brandy, and roasted hens.

On Stage Place jelly mixture in blazer pan of chafing dish. Simmer 5 minutes. Stir in wine and pan liquid. Simmer 3 minutes longer. Pour brandy over and blaze. Serve the sauce hot over roasted hens. Makes 6 servings.

◦§ MENU §◦

Vegetable Juice Cocktail
Rock Cornish Hens with Blazing Wine Sauce
Buttered Lima Beans
Pecan Cake
Tea

TURKEY HASH WITH SPICED CRANBERRY SAUCE

3 tablespoons turkey drippings
2 tablespoons flour
1 cup turkey gravy
½ cup heavy cream
2 cups finely diced cooked turkey

1 cup finely diced cooked potatoes
1 cup cranberry sauce
¼ teaspoon cloves
¼ teaspoon nutmeg

Beforehand If there isn't enough turkey drippings use butter to make 3 tablespoons. Add spices to cranberry sauce.

Tray-Maid Turkey drippings, flour, gravy, cream, turkey, potatoes, and cranberry sauce.

On Stage Melt turkey drippings in blazer pan of chafing dish until they sizzle. Blend in flour until smooth. Gradually stir in gravy and cream, mixing until well blended. Cook, stirring constantly, until thickened (about 8-10 minutes). Blend in turkey and potatoes. Pat them down to make a large cake and brown on one side. Carefully cut down the center of the cake and turn half with a broad spatula. Then turn other half. Brown on other side. Serve with spiced cranberry sauce. Makes 4 servings.

◄§ MENU §►

Mixed Green Salad
Turkey Hash with Spiced Cranberry Sauce
Bavarian Cream
Tea

TURKEY ASPARAGUS CRUNCH

2 cups cubed cooked turkey
1 12-ounce can asparagus tips
or 1½ cups cooked fresh asparagus tips
1 teapsoon celery salt
⅛ teaspoon garlic powder

½ cup turkey gravy
1 10½-ounce can cream of asparagus soup
2 tablespoons dry sauterne
2 cans Chinese noodles
6 brandied apricots

Beforehand   Mix turkey, asparagus tips, celery salt, garlic powder, gravy, and soup. Cover and let stand 2 hours. Heat noodles just before starting.

Tray-Maid   Turkey mixture, sauterne, heated noodles, and apricots.

On Stage   Place turkey mixture in blazer pan of chafing dish. Heat, stirring occasionally, until gently simmering. Stir in sauterne. Cover and heat 10 minutes longer. Serve ·hot over noodles with apricots. Makes 6 servings.

⊷§   MIDNIGHT MENU   §⊶

Champagne Fruit Cup
Turkey Asparagus Crunch
Cheese   Crackers
Café au Lait

GOOD NEIGHBOR TURKEY

½ cup blanched almonds	1 medium onion
1 tablespoon sesame seeds	4 cups chicken broth
½ teaspoon whole cloves	1 large tomato
4 canned chili peppers	1 clove garlic
3 slices dry toast	½ teaspoon ground cinnamon
1 square (1 ounce) unsweetened chocolate	½ teaspoon salt
	12 slices cooked turkey

Beforehand   Grind together almonds, sesame seeds, cloves, chili peppers, toast, chocolate, and onion. Peel and chop tomato and garlic. Mix cinnamon and salt. Remove turkey from bones in large pieces or slice breast meat into thick slices.

Tray-Maid   Ground mixture, broth, tomato, garlic, cinnamon-salt mixture, and turkey slices.

On Stage   Place ground mixture in blazer pan of chafing dish. Gradually stir in broth, mixing until well blended. Add tomato, garlic, and seasonings. Simmer, uncovered, stirring occasionally, for 30-35 minutes, or until slightly thickened. Place turkey in sauce and continue cooking until sauce bubbles gently around turkey and turkey is heated through. Makes 4 servings.

•§ MENU ��•

Good Neighbor Turkey
Hot Rice
Green Beans
Hot Rolls
Greengage Plums with Sour Cream
Coffee   Tea

5.

Love Match —Seafood and Chafing Dish

Brillat-Savarin wrote of seafood as an inexhaustible source of gustatory pleasure, and convincingly discoursed that this delicacy is a source of longevity and amorous desires. Neptune's bounty and the maestro of the table are custom-made, each for the other. The creatures of the deep are best when cooked unhurriedly with quantities of good conversation and then served with smart dispatch.

HADDOCK POACHED IN WHITE WINE

2 pounds haddock fillets
seasoned bread crumbs
¼ cup chopped onion
½ pound mushrooms
2 tablespoons chopped celery

¼ cup butter
1¼ cups dry white wine
¼ cup water
2 tablespoons lemon juice

Beforehand   Cut haddock into serving-size pieces. Wash and drain. Roll fish in seasoned bread crumbs until well covered. Slice mushrooms.

Tray-Maid   Butter, onion, mushrooms, celery, wine, water, lemon juice, and breaded fish.

On Stage   Heat butter in blazer pan of large chafing dish until it sizzles. Add onion, mushrooms, and celery. Cook, stirring occasionally, until lightly browned. Add wine and water. Blend well. Place fish in pan, cover, and simmer 20-25 minutes, or until fish is easily flaked with a fork. Remove fish from pan to warm platter. Add lemon juice to the sauce and cook 2 minutes. Serve sauce over fish. Makes 4-6 servings.

✑ MENU ৵

Frosted Vegetable Juice Cocktail
Haddock Poached in White Wine
Steamed Brown Rice
Watercress and Grapefruit Salad
Coffee Ice Cream with Crumbled Macaroons
Coffee   White Wine

HADDOCK AND RICE ON FRIED TOMATO SLICES

2 cups cooked flaked haddock
1½ cups light cream
¼ pound fresh mushrooms, sliced
1 teaspoon salt
⅛ teaspoon pepper

⅛ teaspoon marjoram
dash cayenne
1 cup converted rice
8 thick tomato slices
seasoned bread crumbs
4 tablespoons butter

Beforehand Mix seasonings. Just before starting, coat tomato slices with bread crumbs and sauté them in the butter. Keep them hot.

Tray-Maid Cream, mushrooms, seasonings, rice, fish, and fried tomato slices.

On Stage Place cream, mushrooms, and seasonings in blazer pan of chafing dish. Heat until small bubbles appear around the edge of the cream. Sprinkle in rice. Cover and cook, stirring occasionally, until rice is tender (it may be necessary to add a little more milk). Add fish and heat until mixture just gently bubbles. Place 2 slices of tomato on each serving plate and spoon rice mixture over them. Makes 4 servings.

◄§ MENU §►

Stuffed Celery   Olives
Haddock and Rice on Fried Tomato Slices
Cherry Cobbler with Hard Sauce
Coffee

SALMON STEAKS À LA COLUMBIA

1 cup chopped cucumber
2 tablespoons chopped onion
2 tablespoons finely chopped celery
1 cup water
3 tablespoons butter
3 tablespoons flour

1 teaspoon salt
1 cup vegetable bouillon
1 teaspoon grated lemon rind
2 teaspoons lemon juice
¼ cup sauterne
4 salmon steaks

Beforehand   Cook cucumber, onion, and celery in the water until tender and then drain. Make bouillon by dissolving 1 vegetable cube in 1 cup hot water. Just before starting, broil salmon steaks and keep them hot.

Tray-Maid   Butter, flour, salt, bouillon, cucumber-vegetable mixture, lemon rind, lemon juice, sauterne, and salmon steaks.

On Stage   Heat butter in blazer pan of chafing dish until it sizzles. Blend in flour and salt. Gradually stir in bouillon, mixing until well blended. Cook, stirring constantly, until thickened. Add remaining ingredients. Simmer 5 minutes. Serve sauce over salmon steaks. Makes 4 servings.

◄§   MENU   §►

Special Tomato Soup Cup
Salmon Steaks à la Columbia
Baked Potatoes
Broccoli au Beurre
Black Bing Cherries in Brandy
Coffee   Liqueur

EGGS AND SEAFOOD SUPRÊME

2 10½-ounce cans cream of mushroom soup
1 cup heavy cream
1 tablespoon cornstarch
2 tablespoons cold water
1 6-ounce can whole mushrooms

6 hard-cooked eggs
18 oysters
1 7¾-ounce can salmon
1 cup dry California white wine
6-8 slices toast

Beforehand Mix soup and cream. Blend cornstarch and water and add to soup mixture. Do not drain mushrooms. Peel and quarter eggs. Drain and flake salmon. Just before starting, make the toast and keep it hot.

Tray-Maid Soup mixture, mushrooms, eggs, oysters, salmon, wine, and toast.

On Stage Place soup mixture in blazer pan of chafing dish. Add all remaining ingredients except wine. Cover and simmer over low heat until edges of oysters curl and oysters get plump. Do not overcook. Add wine and simmer until heated through. Serve hot on toast. Makes 6-8 servings.

◆§ MENU §◆

Sunday Night Supper

Eggs and Seafood Suprême
Broccoli Vinaigrette
Plums in Sherry Sauce
Coffee

SALMON CAKES WITH PICKLE CHIPS

6 medium-size cooked potatoes
1 1-pound can salmon
1 green pepper, finely chopped
1 egg
1 teaspoon seasoned salt
⅛ teaspoon pepper

¼ teaspoon basil
⅛ teaspoon onion powder
fine dry bread crumbs
¼ cup butter
pickle chips

Beforehand Chop potatoes into small pieces. Drain and flake salmon. Mix with potatoes, green pepper, egg, and seasonings and form mixture into 6 cakes. Roll cakes in bread crumbs until well covered. Shake off excess crumbs.

Tray-Maid Salmon cakes, butter, and pickle chips.

On Stage Heat butter in blazer pan of chafing dish until it sizzles. Sauté cakes in butter until browned on one side. Carefully turn and brown on other side. Serve hot, garnished with crisp pickle chips. Makes 6 cakes.

&§ MENU ҙ&

Artichoke-Heart Salad
Salmon Cakes with Pickle Chips
Glazed Carrots and String Beans
Blancmange   Oatmeal Lace Cookies
Coffee

ROSY SALMON FONDUE

1 1-pound can salmon
1 10½-ounce can cream of celery soup
½ cup light cream
¼ pound cheddar cheese

½ teaspoon salt
⅛ teaspoon pepper
¼ teaspoon paprika
toast

Beforehand Drain and flake salmon. Mix soup and cream. Mix seasonings. Make toast and keep it hot.

Tray-Maid Soup, cream, cheese, seasonings, salmon, and toast.

On Stage Place soup, cream, cheese, and seasonings in blazer pan of chafing dish. Heat, stirring frequently, until cheese is melted. Carefully stir in salmon. Cover and heat until simmering. Serve hot on toast. Makes 4 servings.

◄§ MENU §►

Watercress and Orange Salad
Rosy Salmon Fondue
Asparagus Stalks with Lemon Butter
Ice Cream   Macaroons
Coffee

SALMON IN WHITE WINE SAUCE

4 salmon steaks
½ teaspoon salt
⅛ teaspoon freshly ground pepper
4 tablespoons butter
1½ cups California sauterne
½ cup toasted slivered almonds

Beforehand   Wash and dry salmon steaks, and sprinkle them with salt and pepper.

Tray-Maid   Seasoned salmon, butter, wine, and almonds.

On Stage   Melt butter in blazer pan of chafing dish until it sizzles. Place salmon in butter and sauté until browned on one side. Turn and brown on other side. Lower heat and continue to cook until fish flakes easily when tested with a fork. Pour wine over and simmer until heated through. Just before serving, sprinkle with almonds. Makes 4 servings.

◆§   MENU   ȥ◆

Salmon in White Wine Sauce
Shoestring Potatoes
Creamed Spinach
Coupe St. Jacques
Coffee

TUNA CRUNCH

1 10½-ounce can cream of celery soup
⅓ cup California sauterne
1 tablespoon butter
¼-½ teaspoon powdered ginger

½ cup sliced water chestnuts
1 7-ounce can tuna
2 hard-cooked eggs
2 tablespoons chopped parsley
1 can Chinese noodles

Beforehand Mix soup, wine, butter, and ginger. Drain and flake tuna. Peel and chop eggs. Just before starting, heat noodles and keep them hot.

Tray-Maid Soup mixture, water chestnuts, tuna, eggs, parsley, and noodles.

On Stage Place soup mixture in blazer pan of chafing dish and heat for 10 minutes or until mixture gently bubbles. Add water chestnuts, tuna, eggs, and parsley. Simmer until heated through. Serve hot on Chinese noodles. Makes 4 servings.

⋖§ MENU §⋗

Cabbage-Carrot-Raisin Slaw
Tuna Crunch
Butter Beans
Fruit   Cheese
Coffee   Wine

SPAGHETTI WITH WHITE CLAM SAUCE

1 quart clams
1 clove garlic
½ cup salad oil
½ teaspoon white pepper
½ teaspoon salt
1 tablespoon chopped parsley
8 ounces spaghetti, cooked

Beforehand   Drain clams, reserving juice and removing any pieces of shell. Chop clams. Finely mince garlic. Mix pepper and salt. Just before starting, cook spaghetti according to package directions. Drain and toss with 2 tablespoons butter and keep hot.

Tray-Maid   Clam juice, chopped clams, oil, garlic, salt and pepper, parsley, and spaghetti.

On Stage   Place clam juice, oil, garlic, and seasonings in blazer pan of chafing dish. Bring to boil and boil 1 minute. Add clams and parsley. Boil 1 minute longer. Serve hot over spaghetti. Makes 4 servings.

⋰ MENU ⋱

Antipasto
Spaghetti with White Clam Sauce
Tossed Green Salad
Spumoni
Espresso

EASTERN SHORE CRAB RAMEKINS

3 tablespoons butter
2 tablespoons minced chives
4 tablespoons flour
1 teaspoon salt
½ teaspoon dry mustard
⅛ teaspoon paprika
⅛ teaspoon pepper

1½ cups milk
1 3-ounce can chopped broiled
  mushrooms
1 teaspoon lemon juice
3 hard-cooked eggs
2 6½-ounce cans crab meat

Beforehand Mix flour and seasonings. Peel and coarsely chop eggs. Flake crab meat and remove bony tissue.

Tray-Maid Butter, chives, seasoned flour, milk, mushrooms, lemon juice, eggs, and crab meat.

On Stage Heat butter in blazer pan of chafing dish until it sizzles. Cook chives in butter for 2 minutes. Blend in flour. Gradually stir in milk, mixing until smooth. Add mushrooms. Cook, stirring constantly, until thickened. Add lemon juice, eggs, and crab meat. Simmer until heated through (about 15-20 minutes). Serve hot in ramekins or small bowls. Makes 4 servings.

◄§ MENU §►

Eastern Shore Night at Home

Clear Clam Broth
Eastern Shore Crab Ramekins
Buttered Hominy
Collard Greens
Blackberry Pudding with Hard Sauce
Coffee

CRAB AND PEAS À LA CRÈME

3 tablespoons butter
3 tablespoons flour
½ teaspoon salt
⅛ teaspoon white pepper
¼ teaspoon basil
1 cup milk
1 cup heavy cream

¼ cup sherry
1½ cups crab meat *or* 2 6½-
    ounce cans crab meat
1 cup cooked green peas
½ cup slivered almonds
12 buttered toast triangles

Beforehand   Mix flour, salt, pepper, and basil. Mix milk and cream. Flake crab meat and remove bony tissue. Just before starting, make toast and keep it hot.

Tray-Maid   Butter, seasoned flour, milk-cream mixture, sherry, crab meat, peas, almonds, and toast.

On Stage   Heat butter in blazer pan of chafing dish until it sizzles. Blend in seasoned flour until smooth. Gradually stir in milk-cream mixture. Cook, stirring constantly, until thickened. Add sherry, crab meat, and peas. Stir gently to blend. Simmer 15-20 minutes, or until heated through. Just before serving, stir in almonds. Serve hot with toast. Makes 4 servings.

∽§ MENU ℰ∾

Hot Tomato Soup
Crab and Peas à la Crème
Celery and Romaine Salad with Roquefort Dressing
Sliced Oranges and Bananas
Coffee

CRAB MEAT RISSOTO

2 10½-ounce cans cream of mushroom soup
½ cup finely diced green pepper
1 4-ounce can pimiento, diced
2 tablespoons butter
¼ teaspoon nutmeg
2 6½-ounce cans crab meat
2 cups hot buttered rice

Beforehand   Mix soup and nutmeg. Pick over crab meat and remove bony tissue. Just before starting, prepare rice and keep it hot.

Tray-Maid   Butter, green pepper, pimiento, crab meat, seasoned soup, and rice.

On Stage   Heat butter in blazer pan of chafing dish until it sizzles. Sauté green pepper and pimiento in butter for 5 minutes. Add crab meat. Stir in seasoned soup. Cover and heat until simmering. Serve hot over hot rice. Makes 6 servings.

≈§ MENU ईॐ
Bachelor's Dinner

Crab Meat Rissoto
Tossed Green Salad
Fruit   Cheese
Wine   Coffee

NEPTUNE NEWBURG

¼ cup butter
2 tablespoons minced onion
4 tablespoons flour
1½ teaspoons salt
⅛ teaspoon pepper
¼ teaspoon paprika

3 cups light cream
1 6½-ounce can crab meat
2 7-ounce cans tuna
2 tablespoons sherry
2 cups bite-size shredded cereal
¼ cup butter

Beforehand   Mix flour, salt, pepper, and paprika. Flake crab meat and remove bony tissue. Drain and flake tuna. Just before starting, place cereal and ¼ cup of butter in the oven and toast, stirring occasionally, until golden brown. Keep it hot.

Tray-Maid   Butter, onion, seasoned flour, cream, crab meat, tuna, sherry, and cereal bits.

On Stage   Heat butter in blazer pan of chafing dish until it sizzles. Add onion and cook 2 minutes. Stir in seasoned flour and mix until well blended. Gradually blend in cream and cook, stirring constantly, until thickened. Add crab meat and tuna. Cover and heat until simmering. Stir in sherry. Serve hot on cereal bits. Makes 4-6 servings.

⋅§ MENU §⋅

Apple-Nut-Celery Salad
Neptune Newburg
Tomatoes and Zucchini en Casserole
Lemon Bread Pudding
Coffee   White Wine

LOBSTER NEWBURG

cooked meat from 2 lobsters (1 to 1½ pounds each)
or
cooked meat from 1 pound lobster tails
¼ teaspoon salt
⅛ teaspoon white pepper
dash cayenne

3 tablespoons melted butter
½ cup milk
½ cup heavy cream
⅓ cup dry sherry
2 egg yolks
¼ teaspoon salt
4 patty shells

Beforehand Season the lobster with ¼ teaspoon salt, pepper, and cayenne. Mix milk and cream, scald, and stir in sherry. Beat egg yolks with ¼ teaspoon salt and then beat them into the scalded cream. Keep mixture hot, but do not boil. Heat patty shells.

Tray-Maid Butter, seasoned lobster, cream mixture, and patty shells.

On Stage Melt butter in blazer pan of chafing dish until it sizzles. Sauté seasoned lobster in butter until it is heated through. Pour hot cream mixture over lobster meat and heat, stirring constantly, until mixture just simmers. Serve hot in patty shells. Makes 4 servings.

⋖§ MENU ᒾ⋗

Tossed Greens and Tomato Salad
Lobster Newburg
Peas with Garlic Butter
Brandied Fresh Pears with Ginger
Coffee   White Wine

LOBSTER PARMESAN

cooked meat from 2 lobsters (1 to 1½ pounds each)
1 10½-ounce can cream of celery soup
¼ cup light cream
3 tablespoons dry white wine
4 tablespoons grated parmesan cheese
2 tablespoons chopped parsley

Beforehand   Dice lobster meat. Clean and dry shells. Mix soup, cream, wine, and cheese.

Tray-Maid   Lobster meat, soup mixture, parsley, lobster shells or ramekins, and additional cheese.

On Stage   Place lobster meat and soup mixture in blazer pan of chafing dish over low heat. Cook, stirring occasionally, until mixture simmers and lobster is heated through. Just before serving, stir in parsley. Serve hot in lobster shells. If desired, sprinkle with additional parmesan cheese.

◅§   MENU   ɕ▻

Lobster Parmesan
Crisp French Fried Potatoes
Peas with Pimiento and Onions
Endive Tomato Salad
Peaches and Figs with Cream
Coffee   White Wine

SUNDAY SUPPER OYSTERS

1 pint oysters	⅓ cup chili sauce
¼ cup chopped green onion	⅓ cup California dry sherry
⅓ cup chopped green pepper	1 teaspoon soy sauce
⅓ cup chopped celery	dash Tabasco sauce
3 tablespoons butter	½ teaspoon salt
2 tablespoons flour	⅛ teaspoon pepper
1 8-ounce can tomato sauce	toast points

Beforehand   Drain oysters, saving ¼ cup of liquid. Mix onion, green pepper, and celery. Mix tomato sauce, chili sauce, wine, and seasonings. Just before starting, make toast and keep it hot.

Tray-Maid   Butter, onion mixture, flour, tomato-sauce mixture, oyster liquid, oysters, and toast points.

On Stage   Heat butter in blazer pan of chafing dish until it sizzles. Cook onion mixture in butter until soft but not browned. Blend in flour. Add tomato-sauce mixture and cook, stirring frequently, until the sauce boils and thickens. Add oyster liquid and oysters and heat about 5 minutes. or just until edges of oysters start to curl. Do not overcook Serve on hot toast points. Makes 4 servings.

◄§ MENU §►

Sunday Night Supper

Sunday Supper Oysters
Grape-Orange-Avocado Salad
with Creamy Dressing
Milk   Beer

SCALLOPS WITH WHITE WINE SAUCE

1 pound scallops, fresh or frozen	⅓ cup finely chopped green onions
½ cup fine dry seasoned bread crumbs	1 teaspoon salt
¼ teaspoon paprika	⅛ teaspoon freshly ground pepper
¼ cup butter	3 tablespoons dry white wine

Beforehand   Wash and dry scallops. Mix bread crumbs and paprika. Roll scallops in crumbs until well covered. Mix salt and pepper.

Tray-Maid   Butter, scallops, onions, seasonings, and wine.

On Stage   Heat butter in blazer pan of chafing dish until it sizzles. Add scallops, onions, and seasonings. Sauté, stirring frequently, until scallops are lightly browned on all sides (about 15-18 minutes). Place scallops on hot platter. Add wine to butter in pan and simmer for 3 minutes. Return scallops to sauce and keep them hot. Makes 4 servings.

◄§   MENU   §►

Scallops with White Wine Sauce
Shoestring Potatoes
Mixed Fresh Vegetable Salad
Coffee Spanish Cream
Coffee   Milk

LOUISIANA SCALLOPS IN SHERRY TOMATO SAUCE

¼ cup chopped chives
¼ cup chopped green pepper
¼ cup chopped celery
3 tablespoons butter or margarine
3 tablespoons flour
½ teaspoon salt
⅛ teaspoon pepper

dash powdered cloves
dash garlic powder
1 16-ounce can tomatoes
¼ cup California sherry
1 16-ounce package frozen scallops
2 cups cooked rice

Beforehand Mix flour and seasonings. Force tomatoes through a sieve and mix them with wine. Thaw scallops and cut them into pieces.

Tray-Maid Butter, vegetables, seasoned flour, tomato mixture, scallops, and rice.

On Stage Melt butter in blazer pan of chafing dish until it sizzles. Cook chives, green pepper, and celery in butter for 5 minutes. Blend in seasoned flour. Add tomato mixture. Cook, stirring constantly, until sauce thickens. Add scallops. Cover and simmer 10-12 minutes, or until scallops are tender. Serve hot over rice. Makes 4 servings.

⋖ MENU ⋗

New Orleans Dinner at Home

Marinated Zucchini
Louisiana Scallops in Sherry Tomato Sauce
Fluffy Hot Rice
Green Beans with Slivered Almonds
Chocolate Icebox Roll
Chicory Coffee   Wine

SEAFOOD IN PARMESAN SHELLS

1 package pastry mix
3 tablespoons grated parmesan cheese
4 hard-cooked eggs
1 7-ounce can tuna
1 7-ounce can medium-size shrimp
½ cup finely chopped onion
½ cup finely chopped celery

4 tablespoons butter
1 3-ounce can sliced mushrooms
1 10-½-ounce can cream of mushroom soup
1 teaspoon lemon juice
1 teaspoon salt
⅛ teaspoon white pepper
paprika

Beforehand   Prepare the pastry, adding cheese to the dry ingredients, according to package directions. Roll pastry and cut it into 6 circles. Fit circles into tart shells or large muffin cups, and prick them with the tines of a fork. Bake in hot oven (425°) 12-15 minutes, or until lightly browned. Keep them hot or make them a day ahead and reheat. Peel and slice eggs and mix them with tuna and shrimp. Drain mushrooms. Mix soup, lemon juice, salt, and pepper.

Tray-Maid   Butter, onions, celery, mushrooms, egg-fish mixture, soup, tart shells, and paprika.

On Stage   Heat butter in blazer pan of chafing dish until it sizzles. Sauté onion and celery in butter until just tender crisp. Add mushrooms and continue cooking until they are lightly browned. Stir in eggs-fish mixture and soup mixture. Simmer 15-20 minutes, or until heated through. Serve hot in pastry shells. Sprinkle with paprika.

SMOTHERED SHRIMP

2 pounds shrimp	½ teaspoon salt
¼ cup butter	⅛ teaspoon white pepper
1 cup light cream	¼ cup chopped parsley
1 10½-ounce can cream of celery soup	3 cups hot buttered rice toasted almonds (optional)

Beforehand   Shell, devein, wash, and drain shrimp. Mix salt and pepper. Just before starting, boil rice until tender and drain and season it. Keep it hot.

Tray-Maid   Butter, shrimp, cream, soup, mixed seasonings, parsley, rice, and almonds.

On Stage   Melt butter in blazer pan of chafing dish until it sizzles. Add shrimp and stir until it is well-covered with butter. Add all remaining ingredients except rice and almonds. Cover and simmer 20-25 minutes. Serve hot over rice and sprinkle with almonds. Makes 4-6 servings.

◄§   MENU   §►

Smothered Shrimp with Rice
Mixed Fresh Vegetables with Lemon Butter
Fruit Compote with Kirsch
Coffee

GOURMET SHRIMP WITH SPICY SAUCE

2 pounds fresh shrimp or
  2 packages quick-frozen
  shrimp, thawed
4 tablespoons butter
1 teaspoon dried dill weed
	1 clove garlic, minced or
	  crushed
	½ teaspoon salt
	toasted French bread
	spicy sauce*

Beforehand   Wash shrimp. Remove shells and devein. Keep, refrigerated until ready to use. Mix seasonings. Just before starting, toast bread, butter it, and keep it hot. Prepare spicy sauce.

Tray-Maid   Butter, mixed seasonings, shrimp, toast, and spicy sauce.

On Stage   Heat butter in blazer pan of chafing dish until it sizzles. Add seasonings and sauté in butter for 1 minute. Stirring constantly, add shrimp and sauté them until they are just pink. Do not overcook. Serve with toast and spicy sauce.

◄§ MENU §►

Minted Melon-Ball Cup
Gourmet Shrimp with Spicy Sauce
Green Beans with Lima Beans and Pimiento
Celery Hearts   Radishes   Cucumber Sticks
Cheesecake
Coffee

---

* Mix ¼ cup California chablis or other white dinner wine, 1 cup tomato catsup, and 2 tablespoons finely chopped parsley until all ingredients are well blended.

CAROLINA SHRIMP SHORTCAKE

2 cups prepared biscuit mix	1 teaspoon salt
1 teaspoon celery seed	½ teaspoon marjoram
½ cup heavy cream (approximately)	1½ cups milk
	½ cup dry sauterne
¼ cup butter	2 7-ounce cans cooked shrimp
¼ cup flour	crisp watercress

Beforehand Add celery seed to biscuit mix and substitute cream in place of milk when mixing dough. It may be necessary to add an extra tablespoon of cream to make the dough easy to manage. Mix the dough lightly with a fork and spread it in a buttered 8-inch cakepan. Bake in a hot oven (400°) 20-25 minutes, or until done. Split, butter, and keep hot. Mix flour and seasonings. Devein and split shrimp in half lengthwise. Wash and chill watercress.

Tray-Maid Butter, seasoned flour, milk, wine, shrimp, shortcake, and watercress.

On Stage Melt butter in blazer pan of chafing dish until it sizzles. Blend in seasoned flour. Gradually stir in milk and cook, stirring constantly, until thickened. Stir in wine and shrimp. Cover and simmer 15-20 minutes, or until heated through. Spread filling between the layers of shortcake and on top. Serve hot, garnished with watercress. Makes 4-6 servings.

⌐§ MENU §►

Strawberry-Apple-Banana Cup
Carolina Shrimp Shortcake
Asparagus with Lemon Butter
Praline Cookies
Coffee

QUICK SHRIMP CREOLE

1 small onion, finely chopped
2 tablespoons finely chopped
   green pepper
1 clove garlic
¼ cup salad oil
¼ cup flour
1 1-pound can tomatoes

½ cup chicken broth
⅓ cup California sherry
1 teaspoon salt
1 pound fresh shrimp *or* 2
   7-ounce cans shrimp
2 cups hot buttered rice

Beforehand Mix tomatoes, broth, and wine. Devein shrimp. Just before starting, cook rice, season it, and keep it hot.

Tray-Maid Oil, onion, green pepper, garlic, flour, tomato mixture, salt, shrimp, and rice.

On Stage Heat oil to sizzling in blazer pan of chafing dish. Sauté onion, green pepper, and garlic in oil for 10 minutes. Remove garlic. Blend in flour. Add tomato mixture. Cook, stirring constantly, until the mixture thickens. Stir in salt and shrimp. Cover and simmer 10 minutes. Serve hot on rice. Makes 4 servings.

⋖§ MENU §⋗

Quick Shrimp Creole
French Bread
Green Salad
Sponge Cake with Ice Cream
Demitasse   Liqueurs

MANDARIN SHRIMP

¼ cup salad oil	½ teaspoon salt
1 clove garlic	dash freshly ground pepper
2 pounds fresh shrimp or 2 10-ounce packages quick-frozen shrimp, thawed	1 teaspoon gravy improver
	1 14-ounce can pineapple chunks
½ cup chili sauce	1 tablespoon cornstarch
½ teaspoon powdered ginger	buttered thin noodles

Beforehand Peel and cut garlic into pieces. Wash, shell, and devein shrimp. Mix chili sauce and seasonings. Drain pineapple, reserving syrup. Combine syrup and cornstarch. Stir into chili sauce mixture. Just before starting, cook noodles, drain them, butter them, and keep them hot.

Tray-Maid Oil, garlic, shrimp, chili-sauce mixture, pineapple, and noodles.

On Stage Heat oil to sizzling in blazer pan of chafing dish. Cook garlic in oil for 3 minutes. Remove garlic. Add shrimp and cook, stirring occasionally, for 5 minutes. Stir in chili sauce mixture. Cook, stirring constantly, until thickened. Add pineapple chunks and heat thoroughly, but do not boil. Serve hot over noodles. Makes 4 servings.

◄§ MENU §►

Chinese Dinner at Home

Egg Roll with Hot Mustard
Mandarin Shrimp
Buttered Noodles
Chinese Cabbage Salad
Orange Slices with Coconut
Tea

CURRIED SHRIMP MADRAS

1½ pounds fresh or frozen
  shrimp
¾ cup chopped onion
¾ cup chopped celery
¼ cup butter
1 cup tart applesauce
2 10½-ounce cans cream of
  celery soup

1 3-ounce can broiled sliced
  mushrooms
1 tablespoon curry powder
¼ teaspoon salt
assorted condiments

Beforehand Wash, shell, and devein shrimp. Cut them in half lengthwise. Do not drain mushrooms. Mix curry powder and salt. Arrange condiments in serving dishes.

Tray-Maid Butter, onion, celery, applesauce, soup, mushrooms, seasonings, and assorted condiments, such as toasted coconut chips, boiled rice, salted peanuts, diced candied ginger, chutney, and fried parsley.

On Stage Melt butter in blazer pan of chafing dish until it sizzles. Cook onion and celery in butter until almost tender (about 10 minutes). Add all remaining ingredients except shrimp and stir to blend well. Add shrimp. Simmer uncovered, stirring frequently, about 10 minutes, or until shrimps are a delicate pink. Do not overcook. Serve with condiments. Makes 4-6 servings.

◄§ MENU §►

Indian Dinner at Home

Lime Sherbert
Curried Shrimp Madras
Condiments　　Saffron Rice
Vanilla Yogurt with Chopped Pistachio Nuts
Tea

SHERRIED SHRIMP AND EGGS IN POPOVERS

2 tablespoons butter
2 tablespoons finely chopped onion
½ cup finely chopped celery
1 cup cooked fresh shrimp *or* 1 4¾-ounce can shrimp
6 eggs
¼ cup light cream

¼ cup California sherry
1 tablespoon chopped parsley
¼ teaspoon Worcestershire sauce
½ teaspoon salt
⅛ teaspoon white pepper
dash cayenne
4 large popovers

Beforehand Drain and devein shrimp. Beat eggs and mix in shrimp and all ingredients except butter, onion, celery, and popovers. Just before starting, make popovers and keep them hot.

Tray-Maid Butter, onion, celery, shrimp-egg mixture, and popovers.

On Stage Melt butter in blazer pan of chafing dish until it sizzles. Sauté onion and celery in butter for 5 minutes. Lower heat and add shrimp-egg mixture. Cook, stirring frequently, until the mixture is thick and creamy. Split popovers and spoon the mixture into them. Makes 4 servings.

◄§ MENU ৵►

Frosted Sauerkraut and Tomato Juice
Sherried Shrimp and Eggs in Popovers
Potato and Spinach Puff Casserole
Peaches in Burgundy
Coffee

SHRIMP BALLS

¾ pound raw shelled shrimp	¼ teaspoon powdered ginger
1½ slices dry bread	½ teaspoon salad oil
½ teaspoon salt	1 egg
1 teaspoon soy sauce	1 cup beef consommé
½ teaspoon sugar	2 tablespoons chopped parsley

Beforehand Wash and devein shrimp and put them through the fine knife of a food grinder. Then put bread through the grinder. Mix ground shrimp and bread with salt, soy sauce, sugar, ginger, oil, and egg until very well blended and the mixture holds together. This takes from 3-5 minutes. Form mixture into about 24 balls.

Tray-Maid Shrimp balls, consommé, and parsley.

On Stage Bring consommé and parsley to boil in blazer pan of chafing dish. Add the balls, a few at a time, and poach until the balls are dappled a delicate pink. Makes 4 servings.

⊷ MENU ⊶

Shrimp Balls
Creamed Peas and Onions
Chinese Noodles
Pineapple Cheesecake
Coffee

6.

The Provident Impromptus —Cheese and Eggs

With increasing emphasis on simple menus and easy living, expedient egg and cheese dishes are becoming indispensable to today's stay-for-supper menus. This golden couple, always delicate and stimulating to the palate, never heavy or surfeiting, can be teamed separately or together with other foods in the never-ceasing discovery of new dishes (which are sometimes thought to be of more benefit to humanity than the discovery of new stars).

"FRIED" EGGS WITH SOUPER CHEDDAR SAUCE

8 hard-cooked eggs
⅓ cup butter
1 clove garlic, split
½ teaspoon seasoned salt
¼ teaspoon paprika
dash pepper
4 English muffins

1 tablespoon finely chopped
  parsley
2 tablespoons butter
1 11-ounce can cheddar-cheese
  soup
¼ cup light cream

Beforehand Shell eggs while still warm and prick them thoroughly all over with a fork. Mix seasonings. Split the muffins with a fork. Blend parsley into the 2 tablespoons butter. Just before starting, toast muffins and spread them with the parsley butter. Mix the soup and cream and heat.

Tray-Maid Eggs, butter, garlic, seasonings, muffins, and soup-cream mixture.

On Stage Heat butter in blazer pan of chafing dish until it sizzles. Sauté garlic in butter for 5 minutes. Remove garlic and sprinkle in seasonings. Place eggs in seasoned butter and cook, turning constantly, until they are heated through (about 15 minutes). Place an egg on each muffin half and break it open with a fork. Pour hot cheese sauce over. Makes 4 servings.

◄§ MENU §►

Luncheon for a Group of Men

Fried Eggs with Souper Cheddar Sauce
Crisp Vegetable Salad
Strawberries in Port
Coffee   Liqueurs

CURRIED EGGS À LA MAVIS

1 ½ cups sliced scallions
3 tablespoons butter
½ teaspoon salt
dash freshly ground pepper
1 10½-ounce can cream of celery soup

6 hard-cooked eggs
⅓ cup light cream
1 teaspoon curry powder
2 cups hot rice
chutney

Beforehand Cut eggs into pieces. Mix soup, cream, and curry powder. Just before starting, cook rice and keep it hot.

Tray-Maid Butter, scallions, salt, pepper, eggs, soup mixture, rice, and chutney.

On Stage Melt butter in blazer pan of chafing dish until it sizzles. Sauté scallions in butter until tender but not browned. Add all remaining ingredients except rice and chutney. Stir carefully to blend. Simmer 10-15 minutes, or until gently bubbling. Serve on rice and garnish with chutney. Makes 4 servings.

◄§ MENU §►

Curried Eggs à la Mavis
Julienne Raw Vegetable Salad
Hot Buttered Rolls
Pineapple Sherbet
Salted Nuts
Coffee   Tea

JAPANESE EGGS IN ASPARAGUS-SHRIMP SAUCE

8 hard-cooked eggs
1 cup fresh shrimp *or* 1 5-ounce can shrimp
1 10½-ounce can cream of asparagus soup
½ cup light cream
dash soy sauce
3 cups hot buttered rice

Beforehand   Cut eggs into pieces. Wash, devein, and cook shrimp, or drain canned shrimp. Just before starting, prepare rice and keep it hot.

Tray-Maid   Eggs, shrimp, soup, cream, soy sauce, and rice.

On Stage   Mix eggs, shrimp, soup, cream, and soy sauce in blazer pan of chafing dish. Simmer 15-20 minutes, or until heated through. Serve on hot rice. Makes 6 servings.

◄§ MENU §►

Buffet Supper

Japanese Eggs in Asparagus-Shrimp Sauce
Hot Fluffy Rice
Broiled Stuffed Tomatoes
Buttered French Bread
Fresh Fruit Compote Laced with Brandy
Coffee

SWISS MIX

½ pound fresh mushrooms	2 cups light cream
1 green pepper	6 hard-cooked eggs
4 tablespoons butter	½ pound imported swiss cheese
3 tablespoons flour	¼ cup diced pimiento
1½ teaspoons salt	4-6 slices toast
⅛ teaspoon white pepper	

Beforehand   Slice mushrooms. Wash, seed, and slice green pepper. Mix flour with seasonings. Coarsely chop eggs. Shred cheese. Make toast and keep it hot.

Tray-Maid   Mushrooms, green pepper, butter, seasoned flour, cream, eggs, cheese, pimiento, and toast.

On Stage   Heat butter in blazer pan of chafing dish until it sizzles. Sauté mushrooms and green pepper in butter until mushrooms are just tender and very lightly browned. Sprinkle seasoned flour over and mix until well blended. Gradually stir in cream, mixing until smooth. Cook, stirring constantly, until thickened. Add eggs, cheese, and pimiento. Cook until cheese is melted and the mixture is heated through. Serve over toast. Makes 4-6 servings.

◆§ MENU §◆

Swiss Mix
Zucchini and Cucumber Salad
Strawberries in Wine
Sweet Wafers
Demitasse

TORTA CARNE

8 link pork sausages	2 tablespoons butter
1 clove garlic	4 eggs
1 small onion	½ teaspoon salt
4 small tomatoes	dash freshly ground pepper
2 tablespoons butter	corn chips

Beforehand Prick sausages with a fork. Place them in a skillet, cover them with water and simmer gently 10 minutes. Pour off the water. When cool, cut sausages into very thin slices. Cut garlic into 4 pieces. Chop onion. Peel and chop tomatoes. Beat eggs with seasonings until well blended.

Tray-Maid 2 measures of butter, garlic, sausage, onion, tomatoes, egg mixture and corn chips.

On Stage Heat garlic with 2 tablespoons of butter in blazer pan of chafing dish until sizzling. Remove garlic. Stir in sausage slices, onion, and tomatoes. Cook, stirring occasionally, until tomatoes are pulpy and the mixture is thickened. Spoon mixture into a warm medium-size bowl and pour it over egg mixture, blending well. Melt remaining 2 tablespoons of butter in blazer pan. Using a small ladle or small cup, place some of egg mixture in the pan, being sure that you have a blend of egg and sausage. Cook cakes on one side until lightly browned; then turn and brown other side. Serve hot with corn chips. Makes 4 servings.

◅§ MENU ৪▻

Torta Carne   Celery-Romaine Salad
Sliced Oranges with Dates and Coconut
Beer   Coffee

CHINESE SHRIMP OMELET

¾ cup bean sprouts
cold water
1 cup finely diced cooked
   shrimp
1½ tablespoons salad oil

1 tablespoon chopped parsley
½ teaspoon salt
dash pepper
4 eggs
butter

Beforehand Cover bean sprouts with cold water to freshen. Drain well. Mix parsley with salt and pepper and sprinkle mixture over shrimp. Let stand several hours to blend the flavors. Set out eggs and allow to reach room temperature. Do not beat them until ready to prepare omelet.

Tray-Maid Bean sprouts, seasoned shrimp, oil, eggs, and butter.

On Stage Heat oil in blazer pan of chafing dish until it just sizzles. Sauté bean sprouts in oil for 5 minutes. Stir in shrimp. Beat eggs in a medium-size bowl and add bean-shrimp mixture to them. To oil remaining in the pan add about 1 tablespoon butter and heat until it sizzles. Stir egg mixture in the bowl and ladle out one portion into the pan, which should be hot enough to set eggs quickly. When browned on one side, carefully turn with broad spatula to brown other side. Makes 4-6 omelets, depending on size. Serve with fluffy boiled rice.

⋖ș MENU ȝ⋗

Melon Cup
Chinese Shrimp Omelet
Rice
Romaine-Tomato Salad
Almond Cakes   Tea

CANTON CHOP-CHOP OMELET

4 water chestnuts, chopped
4 large fresh mushrooms, chopped
4 tablespoons finely chopped ham
4 tablespoons butter
1 teaspoon soy sauce
6 eggs

Beforehand   Mix chestnuts, mushrooms, and ham. Beat soy sauce and eggs together until eggs are just blended.

Tray-Maid   Butter, ham-vegetable mixture, and eggs.

On Stage   Heat butter in blazer pan of chafing dish until it sizzles. Sauté ham and vegetables in butter 5 minutes. Pour eggs over the hot mixture. Lower heat and cook, stirring occasionally, until eggs are set. Makes 4 servings.

⋅§   MENU   §⋅

Mah Jongg Luncheon

Canton Chop-Chop Omelet
Buttered Crusty Italian Bread
Relish Platter of Crisp Vegetable Bits
Baked Chocolate Pudding with Custard Sauce
Demitasse

EGGS FOO YUNG

½ cup finely diced ham
½ cup thinly sliced onion
¼ cup thinly sliced water chestnuts
1 cup bean sprouts, drained
1 teaspoon soy sauce
6 eggs
2 tablespoons salad oil

Beforehand Mix ham, onion, chestnuts and bean sprouts. Sprinkle with soy sauce and mix well to blend flavors. Just before starting, beat eggs until thick and light (8-10 minutes), and mix them with the vegetables.

Tray-Maid Salad oil, egg-vegetable mixture, and soy sauce.

On Stage Heat oil in blazer pan of chafing dish until it sizzles. With small ladle or cup pour egg-vegetable mixture into the pan, being sure that you have a good blend of vegetables and egg. Cook eggs until lightly browned on one side; then turn and brown other side. Serve with additional soy sauce. Makes 4-6 servings.

◄§ MENU ε►

Teen-Age Supper

Eggs Foo Yung
Fried Noodles
Hot Fluffy Rice
Green Salad
Figs in Orange Juice
Tea   Milk

FOLDED OMELET WITH GARBANZO BEANS

1½ cups canned garbanzo beans	8 eggs
1 small onion, minced	4 tablespoons water
1 tablespoon olive oil	½ teaspoon salt
3 tablespoons butter	¼ teaspoon pepper
	⅛ teaspoon powdered thyme

Beforehand   Rinse beans in cold water and drain well. Then dry well between paper toweling. Mix beans with onion and sauté in oil until onion is golden yellow. Keep hot. Just before starting, beat eggs with water and add seasonings.

Tray-Maid   Bean mixture, seasoned eggs, and butter.

On Stage   Heat butter in blazer pan of chafing dish until it sizzles. Lower heat and pour in eggs. Cook until the omelet is barely set. Then carefully spread hot bean mixture over it and cook 3 minutes longer. Loosen edges of omelet from sides of pan and fold it in half. Makes 4 servings.

◅§ MENU §▻

Friday Supper

Folded Omelet with Garbanzo Beans
Buttered Asparagus
Cheese Biscuits   Butter
Mint Ice Cream over Fresh Pears
Coffee

ROCKY MOUNTAIN OMELET

4 medium-size potatoes, cooked and sliced
8 link pork sausages
paprika
6 eggs
4 tablespoons water
1 teaspoon salt
⅛ teaspoon pepper
chopped parsley

Beforehand Prick sausages with a fork. Place them in a pan, cover them with water, and simmer 10 minutes; then drain, cool, and slice. Just before starting, beat eggs with water, salt, and pepper.

Tray-Maid Sausage slices, potatoes, paprika, eggs, and parsley.

On Stage Place sausage slices in blazer pan of chafing dish over medium heat and sauté, stirring frequently, until lightly browned (about 10 minutes). Stir in potatoes, sprinkle with paprika, and cook until golden brown. Pour eggs over and stir gently to blend. Cook, stirring occasionally, until eggs are set. Just before serving, sprinkle with parsley. Makes 4-6 servings.

⋖§ MENU §⋗

Supper at the Ranch

Rocky Mountain Omelet
Sauerkraut
Shredded Beet and Onion Salad
Frozen Apricot Cream
Sugared Butter Cookies
Coffee

EGGS PIQUANT

2 cups canned tomatoes
¼ cup finely chopped chives
¼ cup finely chopped green
  pepper
1 teaspoon Worcestershire
  sauce
1 cup finely diced cheddar
  cheese

2 teaspoons butter
4 eggs
½ teaspoon seasoned salt
⅛ teaspoon pepper
4 slices rye toast

Beforehand Mix tomatoes, chives, green pepper, and Worcestershire sauce. Cook until thickened (about 25 minutes). Just before starting, make toast, and keep it hot.

Tray-Maid Tomato sauce, butter, cheese, eggs, salt, pepper, and toast.

On Stage Place tomato sauce in blazer pan of chafing dish. Simmer until sauce bubbles gently. Add butter and cheese. Simmer, stirring occasionally, until cheese is melted and well blended. Carefully place eggs on the sauce and sprinkle with salt and pepper. Cover and cook until whites are set and yolks are firm. Serve immediately on toast. Makes 4 servings.

◄§ MENU ‹»

Lunch Before the Game

Eggs Piquant
Artichoke Heart Salad
Butterscotch Pudding
Coffee

EGGS FROMAGE AU VIN

2 tablespoons butter
1 tablespoon chopped chives
1 tablespoon chopped parsley
½ cup dry California white
  wine
¼ teaspoon salt

6 eggs
½ cup grated imported swiss
  cheese
6 slices toast
12 anchovy fillets

Beforehand Beat eggs and mix with cheese. Just before starting, make toast and keep it hot.

Tray-Maid Butter, chives, parsley, wine, salt, egg-cheese mixture, toast, and anchovy fillets.

On Stage Heat butter in blazer pan of chafing dish until it sizzles. Sauté chives and parsley in butter for 5 minutes. Add wine and salt. Blend well. Add egg-cheese mixture to wine and cook, stirring constantly, until cheese is melted and eggs are set. Serve on toast garnished with anchovy fillets. Makes 6 servings.

❧ MENU ☙

Midnight Supper

Eggs Fromage au Vin
Sweet Wafers
White Wine

EGGS ÉLÉGANTE

1 tablespoon butter
1 cup dry white wine
4 tablespoons Roquefort cheese
8 eggs
½ teaspoon salt
⅛ teaspoon white pepper
8 slices toast

Beforehand   Soften cheese. Just before starting, make toast, spread it with cheese, and keep it hot.

Tray-Maid   Butter, wine, eggs, seasonings, and toast.

On Stage   Place butter and wine in blazer pan of chafing dish and heat until butter melts and wine gently simmers (about 8 minutes). Carefully slip in eggs and sprinkle with salt and pepper. Poach eggs in wine until whites are set. Baste tops of eggs occasionally with wine. Drain eggs with a slotted spoon and place them on toast. Makes 4 servings.

◄§ MENU §►

Midnight Snack After a Card Game

Eggs Élégante
Sliced Tomatoes with Chopped Fresh Basil
Beer

SCRAMBLED EGGS AU HAÛT GOURMET

6 eggs	⅛ teaspoon dried rosemary
½ teaspoon salt	2 tablespoons butter
2 tablespoons cream	¼ pound coarsely crumbled
¼ cup California chablis or	bleu cheese
other white dinner wine	1 tablespoon chopped chives

Beforehand Beat eggs slightly. Stir in salt, cream, wine, and rosemary.

Tray-Maid Butter, egg mixture, cheese, and chives.

On Stage Heat butter in blazer pan of chafing dish until it sizzles. Pour in egg mixture and reduce the heat. Cook slowly. As mixture sets, gently lift eggs from the bottom and sides of the pan with a spoon, so liquid can flow to bottom. Do not overcook. Add cheese and chives, while eggs are still creamy. Cook to desired moistness. Makes 4 servings.

◄§ MENU §►

Breakfast at High Noon

Minted Melon Cup
Scrambled Eggs au Haût Gourmet
Brioche
Coffee

SHRIMP AND EGG SCRAMBLE ON PEPPER TOAST

1 3-ounce can sliced mushrooms
1 cup cooked shrimp
3 tablespoons butter
6 eggs

½ teaspoon salt
8 ½-inch slices French bread
2 tablespoons butter, softened
seasoned pepper

Beforehand Drain mushrooms. Devein and cut shrimp in half lengthwise. Beat eggs with the salt. Just before starting, toast bread, spread it with the softened butter, and sprinkle it with pepper. Keep toast hot.

Tray-Maid Butter, mushrooms, shrimp, eggs, and toast.

On Stage Heat butter in blazer pan of chafing dish until it sizzles. Sauté mushrooms and shrimp in butter until lightly browned (8-10 minutes). Pour eggs over, lower heat, and cook, stirring occasionally, until eggs are just set. Serve hot on toast. Makes 4 servings.

◦§ MENU §◦

Sunday Night Supper

Shrimp and Egg Scramble on Pepper Toast
Green Salad
Lemon Chiffon Tarts
Coffee

CHAFING DISH EGGS WITH BACON AND CORN

4 slices bacon
2 tablespoons chopped onion
1 16-ounce can cream-style corn
6 eggs
1 tablespoon Worcestershire sauce
1 teaspoon salt
⅛ teaspoon pepper

Beforehand Cut bacon into small pieces. Beat eggs lightly with Worcestershire sauce, salt, and pepper.

Tray-Maid Bacon, onion, corn, and seasoned eggs.

On Stage Sauté bacon and onion in blazer pan of chafing dish until bacon is crisp and lightly browned. Drain off all but 2 tablespoons of fat. Add corn and simmer 8-10 minutes, or until heated through. Add eggs and cook, stirring gently and constantly, until they are set. Makes 4-6 servings.

◄§ MENU §►

Special Breakfast

Frosted Fruit Juice
Chafing Dish Eggs with Bacon and Corn
Cinnamon Pecan Rolls
Coffee   Cocoa

CHEESE "CAKES"

½ pound swiss cheese, finely
  diced
¼ cup melted butter
2 teaspoons prepared mustard
1 teaspoon salt
¼ teaspoon pepper
1 tablespoon finely chopped
  chives

2 eggs, beaten
1⅔ cups saltine cracker
  crumbs
2 tablespoons butter
watercress

Beforehand Mix cheese, melted butter, mustard, salt, pepper, chives, eggs, and cracker crumbs. Shape mixture into 8 cakes.

Tray-Maid Cakes, butter, and watercress.

On Stage Heat 2 tablespoons butter in blazer pan of chafing dish until it sizzles. Sauté cakes in butter until browned on one side. Turn and brown other side. Serve hot, garnished with crisp watercress. Makes 4 servings.

⊷ MENU ⊶

Luncheon Menu

Cheese "Cakes"
Frizzled Ham
Fruited Coleslaw
Tea Cakes
Spiced Tea

COTTAGE PANCAKES

1 cup sour cream	½ teaspoon salt
1 cup fine curd cottage cheese	4 eggs
1 cup flour	2 cups blueberries
2 tablespoons light brown sugar	2-3 tablespoons butter
1 teaspoon grated lemon rind	Blueberry Cream Topping*

Beforehand Mix sour cream, cheese, flour, sugar, rind, and salt. Beat egg yolks until light and thick (about 5 minutes) and stir them into the cream mixture. Beat egg whites until they form soft peaks and fold them into the batter. Cover and let stand several hours, or overnight. Wash and drain berries. Make topping.

Tray-Maid Pancake batter, berries, butter, and topping.

On Stage Heat butter in crêpe suzette or blazer pan of chafing dish until it sizzles. Pour in about ¼ cup of the batter to make 4-inch cakes. Sprinkle tops generously with berries. When cakes are browned on the bottom and slightly dry on the top, turn and brown other side. Serve hot with topping. Makes about 16 pancakes.

◄§ MENU §►

Breakfast in June

Frosted Fruit Juice
Cottage Pancakes
Crisp Bacon
Coffee

* Wash 1 cup blueberries and place in saucepan with 2 tablespoons powdered sugar and 1 tablespoon water. Cook 5 minutes and cool. Fold into 1 cup sour cream. Chill for several hours, or overnight.

FRENCH CHEESE TOASTWICHES

2 eggs, slightly beaten
¼ teaspoon salt
1 cup light cream
¼ pound gruyère cheese, finely shredded
2 tablespoons mayonnaise

⅓ cup finely chopped stuffed olives
12 ½-inch slices bread
¼ cup butter (approximately)
applesauce

Beforehand   Mix eggs, salt, and cream in deep plate. Blend cheese, mayonnaise, and olives. Spread about 2½ tablespoons of cheese mixture on 6 slices of the bread. Top with remaining slices of bread. Cut each sandwich in half. Just before starting, dip each sandwich in egg-cream mixture.

Tray-Maid   Butter, sandwiches, and applesauce.

On Stage   Heat butter in blazer pan of chafing dish until it sizzles. Sauté sandwiches in butter until golden brown on both sides. Serve hot with applesauce. Makes 4-6 servings.

◄§ MENU §►

Drop by for Brunch

French Cheese Toastwiches
Applesauce
Coffee   Milk

TONGUE RABBIT ON WATERCRESS TOAST

½ cup butter
½ cup flour
2 teaspoons dry mustard
3 cups milk
2 tablespoons Worcestershire
  sauce
dash Tabasco
2 cups grated sharp cheddar
  cheese

2 cups julienne-cut cooked
  tongue
6 slices bread
2 tablespoons butter, softened
2 tablespoons finely chopped
  watercress

Beforehand Blend flour and mustard. Add Worcestershire and Tabasco to milk. Just before starting, toast bread and spread with butter mixed with watercress. If desired, wash and dry additional watercress for garnish.

Tray-Maid Butter, seasoned flour, seasoned milk, cheese, tongue, and toast.

On Stage Heat butter in blazer pan of chafing dish until it sizzles. Blend in seasoned flour. Gradually stir in milk and cheese. Cook, stirring constantly, until mixture is thickened and cheese is melted. Add tongue and heat 5 minutes longer. Serve on toast. Makes 6 servings.

◄§ MENU §►

Informal Buffet Supper

Avocado Tomato Salad
Tongue Rabbit on Watercress Toast
Lime Sherbet
Filbert Cookies
Coffee

CLASSIC WELSH RABBIT

1 tablespoon butter
1 pound sharp cheddar cheese, shredded
½ teaspoon dry mustard
dash cayenne
⅔ cup beer
4-6 slices toast
4-6 slices tomato, fried

Beforehand Open beer and set aside to get flat. When beer is measured, do not count any foam as part of beer. Just before starting, make toast and fry tomato slices. Keep warm.

Tray-Maid Butter, cheese, mustard, cayenne, beer, toast, and tomato slices.

On Stage Heat butter in blazer pan of chafing dish over simmering water. Add cheese and stir until it begins to melt. Sprinkle mustard and cayenne over and blend well. Stir in beer very slowly until well blended. Heat the mixture, stirring constantly, until smooth. Serve on toast and top with slice of tomato. Makes 4-6 servings.

◦§ MENU §◦

Midnight Snack

Classic Welsh Rabbit
Crisp Bacon
Olives   Pickles
Cookies
Coffee

CRUNCHY CALIFORNIA RABBIT

2 tablespoons butter	dash Tabasco
2 tablespoons flour	dash cayenne
1 teaspoon dry mustard	1 cup sliced ripe olives
1 cup dry sherry	2 cups bite-size shredded wheat
1 pound sharp cheddar cheese, grated	2 tablespoons butter
	1 teaspoon powdered basil

Beforehand   Mix flour and mustard. Just before starting, sauté cereal in 2 tablespoons of butter and sprinkle with basil. Keep hot.

Tray-Maid   Butter, seasoned flour, sherry, cheese, Tabasco, cayenne, olives, and cereal bits.

On Stage   Melt butter in blazer pan of chafing dish until it sizzles. Blend in seasoned flour. Gradually stir in sherry. Mix until smooth. Cook stirring constantly, until thickened. Add cheese and stir until melted. Blend in seasonings and olives. Serve on cereal bits. Makes 4 servings.

◄§ MENU §►

Beef Broth on the Rocks
Crunchy California Rabbit
Tossed Green Salad
Frozen Lemon Pudding
Coffee

ROSY MACARONI

2 cups uncooked macaroni
1½ cups grated swiss cheese
½ cup chili sauce
¼ cup water
½ teaspoon seasoned salt

⅛ teaspoon pepper
2 tablespoons sherry
1 tablespoon finely chopped
    parsley

Beforehand Cook macaroni according to package directions and drain. Grate and measure cheese. Mix chili sauce,
water, and seasonings.

Tray-Maid Cheese, seasoned chili sauce, macaroni, sherry,
and parsley.

On Stage Place cheese and seasoned chili sauce in blazer
pan of chafing dish over low heat. Cook, stirring occasionally, until cheese melts. Stir in macaroni, sherry, and parsley. Cover and simmer 10 minutes.

◄§ MENU §►

Hot Sherried Bouillon
Rosy Macaroni
Stuffed Frankfurters
French Green Beans Amandine
Cherry Cobbler
Coffee   Beer

ITALIAN "FRIED" SPAGHETTI

1 clove garlic	1 tablespoon finely minced
8 ounces uncooked spaghetti	onion
4 eggs	¼ cup grated parmesan cheese
2 teaspoons salt	¼ cup butter
⅛ teaspoon freshly ground	¼ cup diced pimiento
pepper	

Beforehand Peel clove of garlic. Cook spaghetti according to package directions and drain. Beat together eggs, salt, pepper, onion, and cheese. Just before starting, mix spaghetti and egg mixture.

Tray-Maid Butter, garlic, spaghetti-egg mixture, and pimiento.

On Stage Heat butter with garlic in blazer pan of chafing dish until sizzling. Remove garlic. Lower heat and stir spaghetti-egg mixture into butter. Sauté, stirring occasionally, until mixture is lightly browned and eggs are set. Just before serving, mix in pimiento. Makes 4-6 servings.

◄§ MENU ৪►

Neapolitan Buffet Supper

Antipasto
Italian "Fried" Spaghetti
Broccoli Vinaigrette
Bread Sticks
Biscuit Tortoni
Italian Honey and Nut Pastry
Espresso

CHAFING DISH SPECIAL

1½ cups uncooked elbow mac-
   aroni
1 cup ripe olive slices
1 cup diced cooked ham
1 tablespoon minced onion
1½ cups light cream

½ teaspoon Worcestershire
   sauce
¼ teaspoon dry mustard
1 cup grated sharp cheddar
   cheese

Beforehand Cook macaroni according to package directions and drain. When preparing ham, set aside some pieces of fat. Add Worcestershire sauce and salt to cream.

Tray-Maid Ham fat, ham, onion, seasoned cream, macaroni, olives, and cheese.

On Stage Heat ham fat in blazer pan of chafing dish until fat is rendered out and sizzling. Sauté ham and onion in fat until lightly browned. Stir in cream and macaroni. Cook, stirring occasionally, until heated through (about 15 minutes). Stir in olives and cheese, mixing gently with a fork. Lower heat and cook until cheese melts. Makes 4-6 servings.

⋅⋅⋅ MENU ⋅⋅⋅

Tomato Consommé
Chafing Dish Special
Avocado and Grapefruit Salad
Chocolate Log
Tea

7.

Hot Salads!

The inventive chef will be enthralled with these unique creations of texture contrasts—warm crispness and succulent tenderness—certainly enough gustatory excitement for one supping experience. These rapidly convenient and savory compounds are guaranteed to still that far-off thunder that threatens the peace fronts on a lazy Sunday evening.

CHAFING DISH CURRIED TUNA SALAD

2 tablespoons sugar	¼ cup vinegar
2 tablespoons flour	2 7½-ounce cans tuna fish
1 teaspoon seasoned salt	½ cup sliced ripe olives
¼ teaspoon curry powder	1 cup shredded carrots
1 cup light cream	crisp potato chips

Beforehand   Mix sugar, flour, salt, and curry powder. Drain and flake tuna fish. Break potato chips into large pieces.

Tray-Maid   Mixed dry ingredients, cream, vinegar, tuna, olives, carrots, and potato chips.

On Stage   Place flour-sugar mixture in blazer pan of chafing dish. Gradually stir in cream. Cook, stirring constantly, until thickened and smooth. Add all remaining ingredients except potato chips and toss gently to thoroughly coat tuna and carrots. Cover and heat just to simmer. Serve hot, sprinkled with chips. Makes 6 servings.

◆§   MENU   §◆

Chafing Dish Curried Tuna Salad
Cherry Tomatoes
Salt Sticks
Butterscotch Chiffon Pie
Demitasse

HOT CREAMY CHICKEN ALMOND SALAD

2 tablespoons flour
2 tablespoons sugar
1 teaspoon dry mustard
1 teaspoon salt
1 cup milk
⅓ cup vinegar

1 tablespoon salad oil
2 cups diced cooked chicken
1 cup diced celery
1 cup chopped salted almonds
Chinese noodles

Beforehand Mix flour, sugar, dry mustard, and salt. Combine vinegar and salad oil. Combine chicken and celery. Open Chinese noodles and heat.

Tray-Maid Mixed dry ingredients, milk, vinegar-oil mixture, chicken-celery mixture, almonds, and heated Chinese noodles.

On Stage Place mixed dry ingredients in blazer pan of chafing dish. Gradually stir in milk. Cook, stirring constantly, until thickened and smooth. Stir in vinegar-oil mixture until well blended. Heat just to simmering. Stir chicken-celery mixture into the sauce and toss lightly to thoroughly coat the ingredients. Cook until celery is tender crisp. Just before serving, toss in almonds. Serve hot on Chinese noodles. Makes 4-6 servings.

◆§ MENU §◆

Minted Citrus Fruit Cup
Hot Creamy Chicken Almond Salad
Toasted Buttered Rolls
Rum Cake
Coffee

HOT CORNED BEEF AND CABBAGE SALAD

2 tablespoons butter
2 tablespoons flour
2 teaspoons dry mustard
1 teaspoon salt
¼ teaspoon freshly ground
  pepper
1½ cups milk

2 tablespoons lemon juice
1½ cups shredded cabbage
1½ cups cooked diced corned
  beef *or* 1 12-ounce can
  corned beef
paprika

Beforehand   Mix flour, dry mustard, salt, and pepper.

Tray-Maid   Butter, seasoned flour, milk, lemon juice, cabbage, corned beef, and paprika.

On Stage   Melt butter in blazer pan of chafing dish. Blend in seasoned flour until smooth. Gradually stir in milk. Cook, stirring constantly, until thickened and smooth. Add lemon juice, cabbage, and corned beef. Toss gently until cabbage and beef are thoroughly coated with dressing. Cook until cabbage is tender-crisp. Serve hot with dash of paprika. Makes 4-6 servings.

◄§   MENU   §►

Clear Consommé
Hot Corned Beef and Cabbage Salad
New England Brown Bread and Butter Sandwiches
Floating Island
Coffee

DUTCH KRAUT SALAD

1 tablespoon salad oil
6 frankfurters
1 19-ounce can sauerkraut
1 teaspoon caraway seeds
1 green pepper

Beforehand Cut frankfurters into ¼-inch slices. Drain sauerkraut. Wash and thinly slice green pepper.

Tray-Maid Oil, sliced frankfurters, sauerkraut, caraway seeds, and green pepper.

On Stage Heat oil in blazer pan of chafing dish until it sizzles. Sauté frankfurter slices in the oil until lightly browned (5-8 minutes). Add remaining ingredients and toss lightly to blend. Heat 5 minutes longer. Serve hot. Makes 4-6 servings.

⊷ MENU ⊶

Dutch Kraut Salad
Dark Rye Bread   Sweet Butter
Muenster Cheese
Mixed Fruit in Wine Compote
Coffee

HAM-A-RONI SALAD

2 tablespoons fat cut from ham	1 teaspoon salt
1½ cups diced cooked ham	dash cayenne
½ cup sliced green onions	3 cups cooked elbow macaroni
¾ cup vinegar	½ cup Italian salad dressing
2 teaspoons sugar	½ cup sliced stuffed olives

Beforehand Mix vinegar with salt, sugar, and cayenne. Marinate macaroni in Italian dressing.

Tray-Maid Ham fat, ham, green onions, vinegar mixture, marinated macaroni, and olives.

On Stage Heat ham fat in blazer pan of chafing dish until only small crisp pieces remain. Sauté diced ham and green onions in fat until onions are tender-crisp (about 5 minutes). Gradually stir in vinegar mixture. Mix well and heat just to simmering. Gently toss in macaroni and olives and mix until thoroughly coated. Cover and simmer 5 minutes longer. Serve hot. Makes 6 servings.

⋖ MENU ⋗

Chilled Tomato Beef Broth
Ham-a-Roni Salad
Hot Buttered French Bread
Fruit in Wine Compote
Coffee

HOT GREEN BEAN SALAD

4 strips lean bacon
1 cup thinly sliced celery
½ cup thinly sliced green onions
4½ cups cooked or canned cut
  green beans

1½ teaspoons seasoned salt
1 teaspoon fresh chopped dill
2 hard-cooked eggs

Beforehand Cut bacon into small pieces. Combine celery and green onions. Drain green beans. Blend salt and dill. Slice hard-cooked eggs and cover to keep from drying.

Tray-Maid Bacon bits, celery, green onions, green beans, blended seasonings, and sliced eggs.

On Stage Sauté bacon in blazer pan of chafing dish until crisp and brown. Remove pieces of bacon and keep them warm. Cook celery and green onions in bacon fat until tender-crisp and slightly glazed (about 5 minutes). Add green beans and seasonings. Toss gently to thoroughly coat beans with dressing. Serve hot, sprinkled with crisp bacon and sliced egg. Makes 6 servings.

◂§ MENU §▸

Pineapple-Melon Cup
Hot Green Bean Salad
Corn Soufflé
Chocolate Icebox Cake
Coffee

NORWEGIAN BEET SALAD

1 29-ounce can sliced beets	1 teaspoon salt
½ cup thinly sliced onion rings	⅛ teaspoon freshly ground
½ cup tarragon vinegar	pepper
½ cup beet liquid	3 tablespoons horseradish
2 tablespoons sugar	sour cream

Beforehand Drain beets and measure ½ cup of liquid. If fresh cooked beets are used, slice to make 3 cups. Slice onions and separate into rings. Mix vinegar with beet liquid. Blend dry ingredients.

Tray-Maid Beets, onion rings, vinegar-beet liquid, mixed seasonings, horseradish, and sour cream.

On Stage Heat vinegar-beet liquid in blazer pan of chafing dish until simmering. Add onion rings, seasonings, and horseradish. Cover and cook 5 minutes, or until onion rings are tender-crisp. Add beets and mix well. Heat again just to simmering, turning occasionally. Serve hot with sour cream. Makes 4-6 servings.

�''§ MENU §⋅

Eggs à la Russe
Salmon Steaks
Norwegian Beet Salad
Hot Rolls
Cheese Cake
Coffee

PENNSYLVANIA DUTCH POTATO SALAD

6 medium-size potatoes
6 slices lean bacon
¼ cup sliced green onion
⅓ cup white vinegar

2 teaspoons sugar
½ teaspoon salt
1 teaspoon celery seed
2 hard-cooked eggs

Beforehand Cook potatoes with skins on until just tender. Drain, peel, and slice while hot and keep them hot. Cut bacon into small pieces. Mix vinegar, sugar, salt, and celery seed. Chop hard-cooked eggs.

Tray-Maid Potatoes, bacon, onion, vinegar mixture, and eggs.

On Stage Sauté bacon and onion in blazer pan of chafing dish until bacon is crisp and onion is lightly browned. Remove bacon and keep it warm. Gradually stir in vinegar mixture and heat just to simmering. Add potatoes and eggs. Toss gently to coat potatoes and eggs with dressing. Just before serving, garnish with crisp bacon pieces. Makes 4-6 servings.

⊷ MENU ⊶

Stuffed Mushrooms
Pennsylvania Dutch Potato Salad
Sliced Ham
Sesame Toast Fingers
Melon with Lime Sherbet
Coffee

HOT RED AND GREEN SLAW

¼ pound lean salt pork
2 tablespoons minced onion
¼ cup wine vinegar
1 tablespoon sugar
1 teaspoon salt

⅛ teaspoon pepper
2 cups thinly shredded green cabbage
2 cups thinly shredded red cabbage

Beforehand Dice the pork. Mince and measure onion. Measure and blend vinegar, sugar, salt and pepper. Wash and thinly shred cabbage; drain well.

Tray-Maid Salt pork, onion, vinegar mixture, and red and green cabbage.

On Stage Dice pork in blazer pan of chafing dish until crisp and brown. Remove from pan and keep hot. Sauté onion in pan 3-5 minutes, or until lightly browned. Add vinegar mixture and blend well. Heat to simmering. Add cabbage. Toss gently to thoroughly coat cabbage with dressing. Cover and heat 5 minutes, or until cabbage is tender crisp. Serve hot, garnished with diced crisp pieces of pork. Makes 6 servings.

◆§ MENU §◆

Hot Red and Green Slaw
Macaroni and Cheese
Petit Fours
Coffee

DELTA RICE SALAD

1 cup uncooked rice	¼ teaspoon freshly ground
½ cup chopped green pepper	pepper
½ cup thinly sliced celery	1¼ cups prepared barbecue
3 tablespoons salad oil	sauce
2 tablespoons flour	¼ cup pickle relish
1 teaspoon salt	sesame seeds

Beforehand Cook rice according to your favorite recipe. Drain well and keep hot. Mix flour, salt, and pepper.

Tray-Maid Hot rice, green pepper, celery, oil, barbecue sauce, seasoned flour, pickle relish, and sesame seeds.

On Stage Sauté green pepper and celery in oil in blazer pan of chafing dish until tender crisp (about 5 minutes). Gradually blend in seasoned flour until mixture is smooth. Blend in barbecue sauce. Cook, stirring constantly, until mixture is thickened and smooth. Toss in rice and relish, mixing gently, until rice is thoroughly coated with dressing. Serve hot. Just before serving, sprinkle with sesame seeds. Makes 6 servings.

◄§ MENU §►

Delta Rice Salad
Broiled Shrimp
Pears in Wine
Coffee

8.

Don't
Let Vegetables
Just Be

'Tis said that the fruits of the kitchen gardens have vast and mystic powers to quicken the course of human vigor, yet they are so often confined to the most unromantic preparation. Imagination makes the earthy carrot an Apollo of vegetables, or a rusty beet a flaming beauty. *Haricot vert, je vous aime.*

ARTICHOKES DIVINE

1 10-ounce package frozen artichokes	1 tablespoon flour
1 cup consommé	½ teaspoon salt
3 tablespoons lemon juice	⅛ teaspoon pepper
4 tablespoons olive oil	pinch sage

Beforehand Thaw and separate artichokes. Mix consommé, lemon juice, and oil. Mix flour and seasonings.

Tray-Maid Artichokes, consommé mixture, and seasoned flour.

On Stage Place artichokes and consommé mixture in blazer pan of chafing dish. Cover and cook 15-20 minutes, or until artichokes are just tender. Sprinkle seasoned flour over, blend, and cook until sauce is slightly thickened. Makes 4 servings.

◄§ MENU §►

Squab Chickens au Vin
Rissole Potatoes
Artichokes Divine
Apple Turnovers
Coffee

GREAT DOWN-EAST SANDWICHES

2 tablespoons chopped onion	2 cups diced cheddar cheese
2 tablespoons butter	6 slices Boston brown bread
1 15½-ounce can baked beans	softened butter
½ cup red wine	chili sauce

Beforehand Just before starting, heat and butter bread. Spread each piece with chili sauce and cut in half. Keep bread hot.

Tray-Maid Butter, onion, beans, wine, cheese, and brown bread.

On Stage Melt butter in blazer pan of chafing dish until it sizzles. Sauté onion in butter until tender and lightly browned. Add beans, wine, and cheese. Heat, stirring occasionally, until cheese melts and mixture is heated through. Arrange three half pieces of bread on each plate and spoon on the scramble. Makes 4 servings.

◄§ MENU ֍

After-the-Football-Game Buffet

Great Down-East Sandwiches
Orange-Nut-Celery Salad
Pumpkin Pie with Whipped Cream Topping
Mulled Cider   Coffee

CREAMED GREEN BEANS AND MUSHROOMS WITH ALMONDS

1¼ pounds fresh green beans or 2 10½-ounce packages frozen French-style green beans
1 medium onion, sliced
1 6-ounce can sliced mushrooms

½ cup sour cream
1 teaspoon salt
⅛ teaspoon white pepper
½ cup toasted slivered almonds

Beforehand Wash and cut fresh beans into pieces lengthwise or thaw frozen beans. Cook beans and onion in enough salted water to cover. Drain. Do not drain mushrooms. Mix cream and seasonings.

Tray-Maid Beans, mushrooms, cream mixture, and almonds.

On Stage Combine all ingredients except almonds in blazer pan of chafing dish. Cover and simmer 15 minutes, or until heated through. Just before serving, sprinkle with almonds. Makes 4-6 servings.

⋙ MENU ⋘

Roast Beef
Yorkshire Pudding
Creamed Green Beans and Mushrooms with Almonds
Raw Vegetable Tidbits
Lady Baltimore Cake
Coffee

GREEN BEANS ORIENTALE

1 4-ounce can sliced mushrooms
1 teaspoon cornstarch
1½ tablespoons soy sauce
1 teaspoon lemon juice
1 5-ounce can water chestnuts
1 1-pound can cut green beans

Beforehand Mix cornstarch and soy sauce. Drain and slice water chestnuts. Drain green beans. Do not drain mushrooms.

Tray-Maid Mushrooms, cornstarch-soy sauce mixture, lemon juice, water chestnuts, and green beans.

On Stage Place the mushrooms, undrained, in blazer pan of chafing dish and heat to boiling. Stir in cornstarch-soy sauce mixture and cook, stirring constantly, until mixture is clear and thickened. Add lemon juice, chestnuts, and beans to mixture. Simmer, uncovered, 10 minutes, or until heated through. Makes 4 servings.

❧ MENU ☙

Cheese Soufflé
Green Beans Orientale
Sesame Seed Rolls
Melon Fruit Compote
Coffee   Milk

HARICOTS AU VIN ROUGE

2 1-pound cans kidney beans
2 tablespoons butter
3 tablespoons chopped onion
3 tablespoons chopped parsley
1 tablespoon flour

1 teaspoon salt
⅛ teaspoon freshly ground
  pepper
1 cup red wine

Beforehand   Drain off all but 1 cup of bean liquid. Mix flour, salt, and pepper.

Tray-Maid   Butter, onion, parsley, seasoned flour, beans, and wine.

On Stage   Melt butter in blazer pan of chafing dish until it sizzles. Sauté onion and parsley in butter until onion is lightly browned. Sprinkle seasoned flour over, blend, and cook until golden brown. Stir in beans and wine. Cover and simmer 25 minutes. Remove cover and simmer 5 minutes longer, stirring occasionally. Makes 4 servings.

⊷§   MENU   §⊶

Baked Fresh Ham
Haricots au Vin Rouge
Tossed Salad
Prune Cake
Tea

BLAZING BEETS

3 cups sliced cooked beets	½ teaspoon salt
2 tablespoons butter	¼ teaspoon pepper
¾ cup water	2 teaspoons light brown sugar
¾ cup orange juice	1½ tablespoons cornstarch
2 teaspoons grated orange rind	¼ cup brandy

Beforehand Drain canned beets or slice fresh beets. Mix water, orange juice, rind, salt, pepper, and sugar and gradually blend in cornstarch. Just before starting, heat brandy.

Tray-Maid Butter, juice mixture, beets, and brandy.

On Stage Heat butter in blazer pan of chafing dish until it sizzles. Gradually stir in juice mixture, mixing until well blended. Cook, stirring constantly, until sauce is clear and smooth. Add beets and simmer 10 minutes, or until beets are heated through. Just before serving, pour brandy over and blaze. Serve just as soon as the flame dies out. Makes 6 servings.

◦§ MENU §◦

Broiled Ham Slice
Baked Sweet Potatoes
Blazing Beets
Hearts of Celery
Ice Cream with Raspberry Sauce
Coffee

CAULIFLOWER SAUTÉ

1 medium size cauliflower
6 slices bacon
1 teaspoon salt
1 teaspoon celery seed
2 tablespoons chopped chives

Beforehand   Cook cauliflower in boiling salted water until tender. Drain and break into flowerettes. Cut bacon into small pieces. Mix salt and celery seed.

Tray-Maid   Bacon, cauliflowerettes, salt mixture, and chives.

On Stage   Cook bacon in blazer pan of chafing dish until crisp and browned. Remove bacon from pan and keep it hot. Sauté cauliflowerettes in bacon fat until lightly browned on all sides. Sprinkle with salt mixture. Just before serving, sprinkle with bacon bits and chives. Makes 4-6 servings.

~§   MENU   §~

Roast Leg of Lamb
Pan Roasted Carrots
Cauliflower Sauté
Fresh Cranberry and Orange Relish
Cream Cake with Bittersweet Chips
Coffee

DUTCH CELERY

4 slices bacon	1 tablespoon wine vinegar
2 cups finely sliced celery	1 teaspoon salt
1 carrot, thinly sliced	½ teaspoon sugar
1 onion, thinly sliced	1 tablespoon chopped pimiento
1 cup consommé	

Beforehand   Cut bacon into small pieces. Mix celery, carrot and onion. Mix consommé, vinegar, salt, and sugar.

Tray-Maid   Bacon, vegetable mixture, consommé mixture, and pimiento.

On Stage   Sauté bacon in blazer pan of chafing dish until crisp and lightly browned. Remove bacon from pan. Add all remaining ingredients except pimiento. Mix well. Cover and simmer 20-25 minutes, or until celery is tender crisp. Serve hot, sprinkled with crisp bacon and pimiento. Makes 4 servings.

⊷§   MENU   §⊷

Roast Capon
Wild Rice Dressing
Dutch Celery
Cherry Pie
Coffee

EGGPLANT VERONESE

1 medium-size eggplant
flour
seasoned salt
4 tablespoons olive oil
6 thick slices tomato
dash oregano
6 slices mozzarella cheese

Beforehand Peel eggplant and cut it into 6 slices. Coat each slice with flour and sprinkle with salt.

Tray-Maid Oil, eggplant, tomato, oregano, and cheese.

On Stage Heat oil in blazer pan of chafing dish until it sizzles. Brown eggplant slices on one side; then turn and place a tomato slice on each browned side. Sprinkle tomato slices with a little oregano. Continue cooking until eggplant is tender. Place a slice of cheese on top of each tomato slice, cover, and heat until cheese melts. Makes 4-6 servings.

✵§ MENU ᢙ✺

Mixed Green Salad
Lamb and Mushroom Kabobs
Eggplant Veronese
Italian Pastries
Red Wine   Espresso

ENDIVE BELGIQUE

4 stalks Belgian endive (bleached)
1 cup sliced celery
2 10½-ounce cans beef consommé
1 cup water
1½ tablespoons cornstarch
1 tablespoon cold water
chopped parsley

Beforehand Wash, trim, and cut endive in half lengthwise. Mix water with consommé. Mix cornstarch with 1 tablespoon cold water.

Tray-Maid Endive, celery, consommé mixture, cornstarch paste, and parsley.

On Stage Place endive, celery, and consommé mixture in blazer pan of chafing dish. Cover and cook until endive is just tender (about 25 minutes). Push endive to one side of pan. Gradually stir in cornstarch, mixing until well blended. Arrange endive in sauce and cook, stirring occasionally, until sauce thickens and becomes clear. Just before serving, sprinkle with chopped parsley. Makes 4-6 servings.

◄§ MENU §►

Bachelor's Dinner

Porterhouse Steak
Shoestring Potatoes
Endive Belgique
Apple Pie à la Mode
Coffee

LEEKS SUPRÊME ON CELERY TOAST

2 bunches leeks
2 tablespoons butter
3 tablespoons flour
1 teaspoon salt
⅛ teaspoon freshly ground
  pepper

1 cup leek liquid
1 cup light cream
½ cup grated sharp cheddar
  cheese
4-6 slices celery toast

Beforehand Wash and trim leeks. Place in boiling salted water to cover and boil for 15 minutes. Drain and reserve 1 cup of liquid. Mix flour with the salt and pepper. Mix cream with leek liquid. Just before starting, make toast, butter it, and sprinkle it with celery salt. Keep it hot.

Tray-Maid Butter, seasoned flour, cream mixture, cheese, leeks, and toast.

On Stage Heat butter in blazer pan of chafing dish until it sizzles. Blend in seasoned flour. Gradually stir in cream mixture, stirring until smooth. Cook, stirring constantly, until thickened. Add cheese and cook until it melts. Place leeks in sauce and simmer until heated through (about 10 minutes). Serve hot on toast. Makes 4-6 servings.

◄§ MENU §►

Citrus Fruit Salad
Salmon Soufflé
Leeks Suprême on Celery Toast
Orange Chiffon Cake
Coffee

OLIVE CHOW YUK

⅔ cup ripe olives
2 medium-size onions
2 cups coarsely sliced celery
1 green pepper
2 tablespoons salad oil
1 cup hot water
¼ teaspoon sugar

¼ teaspoon salt
1 bouillon cube
1 tablespoon cornstarch
1 tablespoon soy sauce
2 cups thin cooked noodles,
   buttered

Beforehand   Cut olives into large wedges. Quarter onions and pull the layers apart. Slice green pepper. Mix water, sugar, salt, and bouillon cube. Mix cornstarch and soy sauce. Prepare noodles and keep them hot.

Tray-Maid   Oil, onions, celery, green pepper, seasoned water, cornstarch mixture, olives, and noodles.

On Stage   Heat oil in blazer pan of chafing dish until it sizzles. Add onion, celery, and green pepper. Cook, stirring occasionally, for 10 minutes. Add seasoned water. Cover and cook 10 minutes longer, or until vegetables are tender crisp. Gradually stir in cornstarch mixture. Add olives, and cook until sauce is clear and thickened. Serve on noodles. Makes 4 servings.

◄§ MENU §►

Egg Drop Soup
Chinese Style Roast Duck
Olive Chow Yuk
Lime Sherbet with Mandarin Oranges
Almond Cookies
Tea

PETITS POIS FRANÇAIS

6 large lettuce leaves	1½ teaspoons sugar
2 pounds fresh young peas	1 teaspoon salt
2 tablespoons finely minced green onion	½ teaspoon pepper
	2 tablespoons butter
1 tablespoon finely chopped parsley	½ cup water

Beforehand   Wash lettuce leaves, but do not dry. Shell peas. Mix onion with parsley. Mix sugar, salt, and pepper.

Tray-Maid   Lettuce leaves, peas, onion and parsley, seasonings, butter, and water.

On Stage   Arrange lettuce leaves to cover bottom of blazer pan of chafing dish. Place peas on lettuce. Sprinkle with onion and parsley and seasonings. Dot with butter. Pour water over. Cover and simmer 20-25 minutes, or until peas are just tender. Makes 4 servings.

◆§   MENU   §◆

Sweetbreads en Brochette
Petits Pois Français
Baked Stuff Potatoes au Gratin
Chocolate Icebox Cake
Demitasse

FRIDAY SUPPER HASH

1 medium onion	1 teaspoon lemon juice
4 tablespoons butter	2 cups cooked diced potatoes
2 teaspoons curry powder	2 cups cooked green peas
2 teaspoons salt	3 hard-cooked eggs
⅛ teaspoon freshly ground	½ cup heavy cream
pepper	1 tablespoon minced pimiento

Beforehand Chop onion. Mix seasonings and lemon juice. Mix potatoes and peas. Chop egg whites and sieve yolks.

Tray-Maid Butter, onion, seasoned lemon juice, potatoes and peas, egg whites, cream, pimiento, and egg yolks.

On Stage Heat butter in blazer pan of chafing dish until it sizzles. Sauté onion in butter until lightly browned. Add seasoned lemon juice and blend well. Add potatoes and peas, egg whites, cream, and pimiento. Blend carefully with a fork. Heat, uncovered, stirring occasionally, 25-30 minutes, or until potatoes are lightly browned. Just before serving, sprinkle egg yolks over the top. Makes 4-6 servings.

◄§ MENU §►

Cheddar-Cheese Soup
Friday Supper Hash
Jellied Fruit Salad with Sour Cream
Coffee   Milk

HAM AND POTATOES OLIVETTE

4 tablespoons butter	2 tablespoons sliced black olives
2 tablespoons minced onion	2 cups diced cooked potatoes
2 tablespoons chopped green pepper	1 cup julienne-cut cooked ham
2 tablespoons sliced stuffed olives	1 teaspoon salt
	½ teaspoon paprika

Beforehand Mix onion, green pepper, and olives.

Tray-Maid Butter, onion mixture, potatoes, ham, salt, and paprika.

On Stage Heat butter in blazer pan of chafing dish until it sizzles. Sauté onion mixture in butter until onion is slightly browned. Add potatoes and ham. Sprinkle with salt. Heat, uncovered, stirring occasionally, until potatoes are lightly browned. Just before serving, sprinkle with paprika. Makes 4 servings.

◅§ MENU §►

Ham and Potatoes Olivette
Apple-Nut-Grape Salad
Cheesecake
Coffee

CHINESE STIR-FRY VEGETABLES

¼ cup salad oil
2 cups sliced Chinese cabbage
½ green pepper
½ red pepper
1 16-ounce can bean sprouts

1 10-ounce can bamboo shoots
1 5-ounce can water chestnuts
3 cups coarsely cut spinach
2 tablespoons soy sauce

Beforehand Slice peppers. Drain bean sprouts. Drain and slice bamboo shoots and water chestnuts.

Tray-Maid Oil, cabbage, green and red peppers, bean sprouts, water chestnuts, spinach, and soy sauce.

On Stage Heat oil in blazer pan of chafing dish until it sizzles. Stir in all ingredients except spinach and soy sauce. Cook, stirring constantly, 8-10 minutes. Cover and steam 5 minutes. Add spinach and soy sauce. Cook until spinach wilts (about 5 minutes). Makes 4-6 servings.

⋅⋅§ MENU ৯⋅

Egg Rolls with Oriental Mustard
Hong Kong Fried Diced Chicken
Chinese Stir-Fry Vegetables
Hot Rolls
Candied Fruits
Tea

PURÉED SPINACH AU CROUTONS

4 pounds fresh spinach *or* 4 10½-ounce packages frozen chopped spinach	1 teaspoon salt
	⅛ teaspoon pepper
	¼ teaspoon nutmeg
4 tablespoons butter	½ cup light cream
2 tablespoons flour	1 cup buttered toast cubes

Beforehand Wash fresh spinach thoroughly and cook until just tender, or cook frozen spinach according to package directions. Drain off excess water and chop fine; then force through a sieve or food mill. Mix flour with seasonings. Make toast cubes and keep them hot.

Tray-Maid Butter, seasoned flour, cream, spinach purée, and toast cubes.

On Stage Heat butter in blazer pan of chafing dish until it sizzles. Blend in seasoned flour. Gradually stir in cream. When well blended, add spinach purée. Cook, stirring constantly, until thickened. Just before serving, sprinkle with toast cubes. Makes 6 servings.

ᵉᔿ MENU ᖰᵉ

Radish Roses   Celery Curls
Broiled Lamb Chops with Kidneys
Crisp Bacon
Puréed Spinach au Croutons
Baked Apple Stuffed with Mincemeat
Tea   Milk

SWEET POTATO PINEAPPLE CAKES

2 pounds sweet potatoes
1 8-ounce can crushed pineapple
1 teaspoon salt
dash pepper
dash nutmeg
1 egg
4 tablespoons butter

Beforehand   Cook, peel, and mash potatoes. Add pineapple with juice, salt, pepper, and nutmeg. Beat in egg. Form mixture into 8 cakes. If mixture is too moist to shape the cakes, cool slightly.

Tray-Maid   Potato cakes and butter.

On Stage   Heat butter in blazer pan of chafing dish until it sizzles. Brown cakes on both sides in butter. This takes 5-8 minutes for each side. Makes 4 servings.

◄§ MENU §►

Tongue with Horseradish Sauce
Sweet Potato-Pineapple Cakes
Buttered Cabbage
Lemon Meringue Pie
Coffee

GREEN TOMATOES PARMESAN

6 medium-size green tomatoes
½ cup flour
1 teaspoon seasoned salt
¼ teaspoon pepper
5 tablespoons butter
grated parmesan cheese

Beforehand Wash and cut tomatoes into ½-inch slices. Mix flour and seasonings. Just before starting, coat tomato slices well with seasoned flour.

Tray-Maid Butter, tomato slices, and cheese.

On Stage Heat butter in blazer pan of chafing dish until it sizzles. Sauté tomato slices until browned on both sides. Just before serving, sprinkle generously with cheese. Makes 4-6 servings.

◆§ MENU §◆

Clam Chowder
Swordfish Steaks au Meunière
Potatoes in Jackets
Green Tomatoes Parmesan
Gingerbread with Hot Applesauce
Coffee

SPICY YAM CHIPS

4 medium-size yams or sweet potatoes
2 cups water
2 cups light brown sugar
2 tablespoons butter

1 tablespoon grated orange rind
¼ teaspoon nutmeg
¼ teaspoon ground cloves
1 teaspoon salt

Beforehand Parboil yams 15-20 minutes, or until just tender. Cool, peel, and cut into slices. Mix water, sugar, butter, orange rind, and seasonings.

Tray-Maid Spiced sugar mixture and sliced yams.

On Stage Place sugar mixture in blazer pan of chafing dish and bring to a boil over high heat. Drop yam slices into syrup. Cook, covered, for 20 minutes, turning occasionally. Remove cover and cook until slices are glazed and transparent. Baste slices frequently during last 5 minutes of cooking. Makes 4-6 servings.

❧ MENU ☙

Roast Turkey with Chestnut Dressing
Spicy Yam Slices
Brussels Sprouts
Mushroom Creamed Onions
Hearts of Celery   Radishes
Baked Pears with Orange Sauce
Champagne   Coffee

YAM RUMMIES

6 medium-size yams
1 cup firmly packed brown sugar
1 cup water
4 tablespoons butter
⅓ cup dark rum

Beforehand   Parboil yams until just tender. Cool, peel, and cut in half lengthwise. Mix sugar and water.

Tray-Maid   Butter, sugar mixture, yams, and rum.

On Stage   Heat butter in blazer pan of chafing dish until it sizzles. Add sugar-water mixture. Blend well. Bring to a boil. Add rum. Arrange yams in syrup and cook uncovered, basting frequently until yams are glazed. Makes 4-6 servings.

◄§   MENU   §►

Roast Loin of Pork
Yam Rummies
Broccoli Hollandaise
Bib Lettuce Salad
Snow Pudding
Coffee

ZINGY ZUCCHINI

1½ pounds zucchini	½ teaspoon oregano
3 tablespoons butter	½ teaspoon sugar
1 teaspoon seasoned salt	1 cup sour cream
⅛ teaspoon pepper	2 tablespoons lemon juice

Beforehand   Wash and cut zucchini into thin slices. Mix all remaining ingredients except butter.

Tray-Maid   Butter, zucchini, and sour cream mixture.

On Stage   Heat butter in blazer pan of chafing dish until it sizzles. Sauté zucchini slices in butter until lightly browned (about 10 minutes). Cover and steam about 15 minutes, or until just tender. Pour sour cream mixture over. Cover and simmer 5 minutes longer, or until heated through. Makes 4-6 servings.

◄§ MENU §►

Veal Scaloppine
Spaghetti with Butter
Zingy Zucchini
Marrons Glacés
Coffee

9.

Spectacular
Desserts

There is an old Epicurean proverb, "As they eat, so will your guests love you." Gastronomical pleasure is such that inevitably the grand finale of a meal lingers in the memory of the diner. Armed with this knowledge, no hostess can invite the least reproach for a slip-of-menu, so long as the dessert is an exquisite masterpiece. Long live the blazing fruits and succulent custards that bring down the dinner curtain.

189

POMMES D'AMOUR

3 large tart apples
2 tablespoons lemon juice
½ cup brown sugar, firmly
  packed
1 teaspoon cinnamon

1 teaspoon nutmeg
⅓ cup butter
1 jigger apple brandy
whipped cream

Beforehand Wash and core apples. Cut into ½-inch slices. Sprinkle with lemon juice. Mix sugar and spices. Heat brandy.

Tray-Maid Butter, apple slices, spiced sugar, brandy, and whipped cream.

On Stage Heat butter in blazer pan of chafing dish until it sizzles. Place a few apple slices in the pan. Sprinkle each slice with 1 teaspoon spiced sugar mixture. Sauté slices on one side until lightly browned; then turn and sprinkle other side with spiced sugar. Cook 5 minutes longer, or until fork tender. Keep cooked slices warm while continuing to cook remaining slices. Return slices to the pan, pour brandy over and blaze. Serve hot with whipped cream. Makes 4 servings.

⊷§ MENU ৡ⊷

Beef Broth on the Rocks with Lime
Beef Stroganoff
Green Noodles
Zucchini Stewed with Tomatoes
Pommes d'Amour
Demitasse

BLAZING BERRY BINGE

1 pint strawberries
1 pint blueberries
1 pint raspberries
1 cup sugar
¾ cup water
½ cup apricot brandy

Beforehand Wash and pick over berries. Stem strawberries and keep them whole. Mix berries and sugar. Cover and let stand 1 hour. Heat brandy.

Tray-Maid Berries, water, and brandy.

On Stage Place berries in blazer pan of chafing dish. Pour water over. Gradually bring berries to a gentle boil. Lower heat and simmer 5 minutes. Pour brandy over and blaze. Serve warm over meringue shells, angel cake, vanilla ice cream, and so forth.

◄§ MENU §►

Fourth of July Supper

Spaghetti with White Clam Sauce
Wilted Spinach and Bacon Salad
Cheese-Bread Toast
Blazing Berry Binge
Coffee   Wine

BLUEBERRY DEW

1 pint blueberries
2 tablespoons lemon juice
¾ cup sugar
½ cup water
2 cups prepared biscuit mix

3 tablespoons sugar
1 teaspoon nutmeg
¾ cup light cream
hard sauce

Beforehand   Wash and pick over berries. Mix with lemon juice, sugar, and water. Blend biscuit mix, 3 tablespoons sugar, and nutmeg. Just before starting, blend in cream and mix lightly with a fork. Do not over-mix.

Tray-Maid   Blueberries, dumpling dough, and hard sauce.

On Stage   Place blueberry mixture in blazer pan of chafing dish. Cover and simmer about 5 minutes, or until berries are just soft. Drop spoonfuls of dumpling dough onto cooked berries. Cover and simmer 15-18 minutes, or until dumplings are dry on top. Serve hot with iced hard sauce. Makes 6 servings.

◄§   MENU   §►

Stuffed Eggs with Cucumber Mayonnaise
Ham Loaf with Sherry Sauce
Stuffed Baked Potatoes
Mixed Green Salad
Blueberry Dew
Coffee

BLAZING FIGS

½ cup unsweetened pineapple juice
⅓ cup orange juice
2 tablespoons lime juice
½ cup sugar
12 fresh white figs
½ cup brandy
shredded almonds

Beforehand Mix juices and sugar. Wash and thoroughly dry figs. Just before starting, heat brandy.

Tray-Maid Juice mixture, figs, brandy, and almonds.

On Stage Place juice mixture in blazer pan of chafing dish and heat until mixture just simmers. Place figs in the syrup, lower the heat, and cook, turning figs occasionally, until they are transparent (about 25 minutes). It may be necessary to add a little more pineapple juice to prevent sticking. Pour brandy over and blaze. Serve hot sprinkled with almonds.

◄§ MENU ৡ►

Make Ahead Dinner Party

Pot Roast with Vegetables
Curried Celery Root Salad
Blazing Figs
Coffee

FRUITED CHARLOTTE FLAMBÉE

½ cup diced fresh pineapple
½ cup fresh or frozen black
   bing cherries, pitted
½ cup diced fresh pears
½ cup orange sections

¼ cup lemon juice
1 cup apricot jam
½ cup light rum
6 slices sponge cake

Beforehand Mix fruits with lemon juice and jam. Cover and let stand 1 hour or more. Just before starting, heat rum.

Tray-Maid Fruits, rum, and cake.

On Stage Place fruit in blazer pan over low heat and gradually bring to a simmer. Stir occasionally to prevent sticking. Simmer 5 minutes. Pour rum over and blaze. Serve hot fruit over sponge cake. Makes 6 servings.

⋖§ MENU §⋗

After-Theatre Dessert

Fruited Charlotte Flambée
Coffee   Sanka

ICE CREAM SUPRÊME

1 quart prepared eggnog
1½ tablespoons cornstarch
1 cup diced candied fruit
½ cup brandy
1½ quarts vanilla ice cream

Beforehand Blend ¼ cup of eggnog into cornstarch to make a smooth paste. Gradually stir paste into remaining eggnog. Marinate fruit in ¼ cup of brandy. Measure another ¼ cup and heat just before starting.

Tray-Maid Eggnog mixture, brandied fruit, brandy, and ice cream.

On Stage Heat eggnog in blazer pan of chafing dish until mixture simmers and thickens. Stir constantly. Add fruits and simmer 5 minutes. Pour brandy over the sauce and blaze. Serve warm over ice cream. Makes 8 servings.

◄§ MENU §►

Birthday Party for a Man

Charcoal Broiled Steak
Scalloped potatoes
Tomato Salad
Ice Cream Suprême
Coffee

MACAROON FRUIT CREAM

½ cup sugar
¼ cup flour
dash salt
2 eggs
2 cups light cream
1 teaspoon vanilla

¼ cup almond macaroon
  crumbs
1 tablespoon finely diced candied orange peel
1 tablespoon finely diced candied cherries

Beforehand   Mix sugar, flour, and salt. Stir in eggs, mixing until smooth. Gradually beat in cream. Mix crumbs and fruits.

Tray-Maid   Sugar-cream mixture, vanilla, and crumb-fruit mixture.

On Stage   Place sugar-cream mixture in blazer pan of chafing dish over hot water. Cook, stirring constantly, until thickened and smooth (15-20 minutes). Add vanilla and crumb-fruit mixture. Blend well. Serve hot. Makes 6 servings.

✺§   MENU   ॐ▸

Pork Chops with Mushroom Gravy
Sherried Sweet Potatoes
Pineapple and Mixed Green Salad
Macaroon Fruit Cream
Coffee

KENTUCKY DERBY NECTARINES FLAMBÉE

1½ cups water
1 cup sugar
dash salt
1 1-inch piece lemon rind
8 nectarines
½ cup bourbon

Beforehand Mix water, sugar, salt, and lemon rind. Let stand several hours. Just before starting, peel nectarines, cut them in half, and remove the stones. Heat bourbon.

Tray-Maid Sugar mixture, nectarines, and bourbon.

On Stage Heat sugar mixture in blazer pan of chafing dish until mixture boils and sugar is dissolved. Simmer 5 minutes. Add nectarines and simmer 10 minutes longer. Remove lemon rind. Just before serving, pour bourbon over and flame. Serve immediately. Makes 4-6 servings.

◄§ MENU §►

Tossed Salad
Steak au Poivre
Stuffed Mushrooms
Hot Potato Chips
Kentucky Derby Nectarines Flambée
Coffee

MONT BLANC BRANDIED ORANGES

6 oranges
2 cups water
1 cup sugar
¾ cup brandy
6 whole cloves
2 cups small curd cottage
cheese

½ cup sugar
1 tablespoon lemon juice
1 tablespoon grated orange
rind

Beforehand   Wash and section oranges. Blend water, 1 cup sugar, ½ cup of brandy, and cloves. Set aside remaining brandy. Force cottage cheese through a fine sieve and beat in ½ cup of sugar, lemon juice, and rind. Pile lightly in serving dish and chill.

Tray-Maid   Orange sections, water-sugar mixture, ¼ cup brandy, and cheese mixture.

On Stage   Place orange sections and water-sugar mixture in blazer pan of chafing dish. Simmer 10 minutes. Remove cloves. Pour brandy over and blaze. Serve immediately over cheese. Makes 6-8 servings.

⋳§   MENU   ⋲⋗

Frosted Clam Juice
Fillet of Sole Meunière
Shoestring Potatoes
Cucumber Salad
Mont Blanc Brandied Oranges
Tea

SHERRIED PEACHES

¼ cup dark brown sugar, firmly packed
½ cup light corn syrup
⅓ cup sherry
2 tablespoons butter
1 29-ounce can cling peach halves
sour cream

Beforehand   Mix sugar, syrup, and wine. Drain peaches.

Tray-Maid   Sugar mixture, butter, peaches, and sour cream.

On Stage   Place sugar mixture and butter in blazer pan of chafing dish and simmer over medium heat 5 minutes. Add peaches. Turn off heat and let stand 5 minutes, turning peaches several times. Serve warm with sour cream. Makes 5-6 servings.

⊷ MENU ⊶

Broiled Ham Slice
Creamed Spinach
Potato Puffs
Sherried Peaches
Petit Fours
Coffee

PEACHES 'N' CREAM

6 large ripe peaches
2 tablespoons butter
1 cup light brown sugar, firmly packed
½ cup heavy cream
¼ cup light rum

Beforehand Peel and halve peaches. Cover with lightly salted water to keep from darkening. Just before starting, remove peaches from water and pat them dry.

Tray-Maid Butter, brown sugar, peaches, cream, and rum.

On Stage Heat butter in blazer pan of chafing dish until it sizzles. Sprinkle in sugar and stir until well blended. Place peach halves in sugar and turn to coat all sides. Cover and simmer, turning and basting often, until peaches are tender (about 25 minutes). Pour cream and rum over and bring to a boil. Serve hot. Makes 4-6 servings.

◄§   MENU   §►

Rock Cornish Game Hens
Brown Rice with Red and Green Peppers
Petits Pois with Onion
Peaches and Cream
Chocolate-Filled Cookies
Wine
Demitasse

ROSY CLARET-POACHED PEACHES

6 large ripe peaches
1 cup claret
1 cup sugar
1 stick cinnamon
3 whole cloves

Beforehand Plunge peaches into hot water for a few seconds. Then place them in cold water. Peel, cut in half, and remove stones. Save 3 of the stones. Place peach halves in lightly salted water until ready to use. This prevents peaches from darkening. Mix remaining ingredients. Drain peaches just before starting.

Tray-Maid Spiced wine mixture, peach stones, and peaches.

On Stage Place spiced wine mixture and peach stones in blazer pan of chafing dish and simmer 5 minutes, or until sugar is dissolved. Place peach halves in wine and poach, basting occasionally, until fruit is tender (25-30 minutes). Serve warm with wine liquid. Makes 4 servings.

ᚖ MENU ᚖ

Grapefruit Salad
Baked Bean Casserole
Brown Bread
Rosy Claret-Poached Peaches
Coffee

POIRES AU CHOCOLAT

12 halves, fresh, cooked, *or*
  canned pears
4 squares (4 ounces) unsweetened chocolate
½ cup cocoa

2 cups sour cream
3 cups sugar
2 teaspoons vanilla
¼ cup crème de cacao
dash salt

Beforehand   Drain pears and keep cold. Break chocolate into pieces. Mix cocoa, sour cream, and sugar.

Tray-Maid   Chocolate, cocoa mixture, vanilla, crème de cacao, salt, and pears.

On Stage   Place chocolate and cocoa mixture in blazer pan of chafing dish. Stir to blend. Cook, stirring occasionally, until thickened and smooth (25-30 minutes). Add vanilla, crème de cacao, and salt. Blend well. Serve hot over chilled pears. Makes 6 servings.

✑§ MENU ?✎

Bridge Dessert

Poires au Chocolat
Petit Fours
Coffee   Tea

POIRES À LA CRÈME

6 ripe Bartlett pears
½ cup butter
3 tablespoons brown sugar
⅓ cup dark rum
1½ cups heavy cream

Beforehand Peel and core pears. Place them in lightly salted water until ready to use. Just before starting, drain pears, pat them dry, and cut them into large cubes.

Tray-Maid Butter, pears, sugar, rum, and cream.

On Stage Melt butter in blazer pan of chafing dish until it sizzles. Sauté pears in butter until lightly browned on all sides. Sprinkle with sugar and rum. Simmer until liquid in the pan has been almost absorbed. Pour cream over and heat until gently simmering (about 5 minutes). Makes 4-6 servings.

◆§ MENU ੩◆

Sliced Meats
Potato Salad
French Bread
Poires à la Crème
Demitasse   Wine

HONIED PINEAPPLE À LA NERO

1 large ripe pineapple
1 cup orange blossom honey
¼ cup orange curaçao
2 ounces dark rum

Beforehand Peel, core, and slice pineapple. Arrange slices in blazer pan of chafing dish. Pour honey and curaçao over, being sure that all pieces are covered with the liquid. Cover and let stand 1 hour. Just before starting, heat rum.

Tray-Maid Pineapple and rum.

On Stage Place blazer pan over low heat and gradually bring pineapple to a simmer. Cook 5 minutes, turning slices once. Pour warm rum over and blaze. Serve hot. Makes 6 servings.

◄§ MENU §►

Shower Luncheon

Jellied Chicken Salad
Macaroni, Mushroom Soup, and Cheese Casserole
Hot Rolls
Honied Pineapple à la Nero
Coffee   Rosé Wine

SNOW PEAK PUDDING

4 eggs	¼ teaspoon vanilla
dash salt	¼ teaspoon rum flavoring
½ cup sugar	nutmeg
2 cups milk	currant jelly

Beforehand Let eggs stand at room temperature for 1 hour. Then separate yolks from whites. Just before starting, beat egg whites with salt until soft peaks are formed. Then gradually beat in ¼ cup of the sugar until the meringue is stiff. Heat milk just to boiling. Beat egg yolks with vanilla, rum flavoring, and remaining sugar until thick.

Tray-Maid Hot milk, meringue, paper toweling, egg yolks, nutmeg, and jelly.

On Stage Place boiling milk in blazer pan of chafing dish over low heat. Drop tablespoons of meringue into milk and poach, turning once, until set. Drain on several thicknesses of paper toweling. Add some of hot milk to egg yolks and then stir mixture into the milk in the pan. Cook, stirring constantly, until custard coats the spoon. Put peaks into serving dishes and pour custard over. Garnish with sprinkling of nutmeg and jelly. Makes 6-8 servings.

◄§ MENU §►

Dessert Party

Snow Peak Pudding
Chocolate-Filled Cookies
Spiced Tea

FLAMING SULTANAS

1 large bunch sultana raisins
1½ cups cognac

Beforehand   Just before starting, heat cognac.

Tray-Maid   Sultanas and cognac.

On Stage   Place ¼ cup of cognac with raisins in blazer pan of chafing dish over low heat. When warm, pour remaining cognac over. Blaze and keep ladling the burning liquor over the raisins until the flame goes out. Let guests serve themselves to this delicious tidbit.

◄§   MENU   §►

Sherried Consommé
Persian Green Sauce over Rice
Sesame Seed Rolls
Flaming Sultanas   Crackers
Coffee   Wine

STRAWBERRY OMELET

1 pint strawberries
¼ cup powdered sugar
2 tablespoons apricot brandy
6 eggs
¾ teaspoon salt
2 tablespoons butter

Beforehand   Wash and hull berries. Cut in half and sprinkle with sugar. Pour brandy over. Cover and let stand several hours. Beat eggs with salt until yolks and whites are just blended. Drain berries and reserve juice.

Tray-Maid   Butter, eggs, strawberries, and strawberry juice.

On Stage   Heat butter in blazer pan of chafing dish until it sizzles. Lower the heat and pour in egg mixture. As sides of eggs set, loosen from the pan and carefully tilt to let the uncooked egg run under the cooked portion. Continue cooking until omelet is just set. Spoon berries on one half of omelet, and fold over other half. Serve with strawberry juice. Makes 4 servings.

◄§ MENU §►

Festive Supper

Lobster Chowder
Pilot Biscuits
Strawberry Omelet
Coffee

TIPSY TANGERINES

8 tangerines	4 cinnamon sticks
1¼ cups water	½ cup sweet sauterne
½ cup sugar	1 tablespoon lemon juice
1 whole nutmeg	1 jigger Triple Sec
6 whole cloves	1½ quarts vanilla ice cream

Beforehand Wash fruit, peel, and remove thin strings and seeds. Put aside the peel from 3 of the tangerines. Separate fruit into sections. Mix water and sugar. Tie spices in a small cheesecloth bag. Mix wine and lemon juice. Keep ice cream frozen until ready to use.

Tray-Maid Tangerine peel, water-sugar mixture, spice bag, wine-lemon mixture, tangerine sections, Triple Sec, and ice cream.

On Stage Place tangerine peel, water-sugar mixture, and spice bag in blazer pan of chafing dish. Simmer for 10 minutes. Remove peel and spice bag. Add tangerine sections and wine. Simmer 10 minutes. Just before serving, pour Triple Sec over and blaze. Serve over ice cream. Makes 8-10 servings.

◆§ MENU §◆

Curried Green Pea Soup with Ham
Buttered Hard Rolls
Mixed Green Salad
Tipsy Tangerines
Coffee

MADEIRA ANGELS

6 egg yolks
¼ cup sugar
3 tablespoons orange juice
1 tablespoon lemon juice
¾ cup madeira
6 1-inch slices angel cake

Beforehand   Beat egg yolks until thick and lemon-colored (about 5 minutes). Gradually beat in remaining ingredients. Do this a few minutes before starting to make sauce.

Tray-Maid   Egg-wine mixture and angel cake.

On Stage   Place egg-wine mixture in blazer pan of chafing dish over hot water. Do not let water boil. Cook, stirring constantly, until mixture thickens. Do not overcook or the sauce will curdle. Serve hot over pieces of angel cake. Makes 6 servings.

◄§   MENU   §►

Backyard Picnic

Boullion on the Rocks
Turkey-Ham Sandwiches
Tuna Salad Sandwiches
Pickles
Potato Chips
Madeira Angels
Iced Coffee

MOCHA SOUFFLÉ

4 ounces German's sweet chocolate
½ cup milk
⅔ cup strong coffee
2 tablespoons sugar
⅛ teaspoon salt
1 teaspoon vanilla
3 eggs

Beforehand   Break chocolate into pieces. Blend together milk and coffee. Have eggs at room temperature.

Tray-Maid   Chocolate, milk-coffee mixture, sugar, salt, vanilla, and eggs.

On Stage   Place chocolate and milk-coffee mixture in blazer pan of chafing dish over hot water. Beat with small wire whisk or fork until chocolate is melted and mixture is smooth. Add sugar salt, and vanilla. Beat until well blended. Beat eggs until very light and fluffy. Lightly mix into chocolate mixture. Cover and cook over hot water without lifting cover for 20 minutes. Remove from heat and serve immediately. Makes 4 servings.

◆§   MENU   §◆

Stuffed Squab Chickens with Ham
Rice Pilaf
Glazed Carrots
Marinated Sprigs of Watercress Salad
Mocha Soufflé
Demitasse

ZABAGLIONE AU GRAND MARNIER

6 egg yolks
2 tablespoons sugar
½ cup Grand Marnier

Beforehand A small wire whisk is a good tool to use in making this light fluffy dessert. The water should just simmer at all times during the cooking; never let it boil. Have egg yolks at room temperature.

Tray-Maid Egg yolks, sugar, and Grand Marnier.

On Stage Place ingredients in blazer pan of chafing dish. Beat together until well blended. Place blazer pan over medium-hot water in water pan. Begin to beat immediately. If mixture looks grainy, remove from heat and beat until smooth again. Return to heat and beat constantly until custard puffs up high and thickens. When custard begins to hold its shape, remove from heat and serve in glasses. Makes 4-6 servings.

⊷§ MENU ৡৡ

Chef's Salad
Hot Rolls   Butter
Zabaglione au Grand Marnier
Demitasse

10.

Rousing
After-Dinner
Beverages

Bobbets, punches, chocolates, and coffees—what heady brews are these steaming beverages! Here are fluid, flaming creations destined to lift the dome of dinner drowsiness and reunite surfeited humans with the gods of wit and laughter.

SPICED ALE

3 bottles ale
¼ teaspoon whole cloves
¼ teaspoon mace
¼ teaspoon ginger
2 tablespoons sugar
1 large lemon
dash baking soda

Beforehand Mix spices with sugar. Squeeze lemon and strain the juice.

Tray-Maid Ale, spiced sugar, lemon juice, and baking soda.

On Stage Place ale and spiced sugar in blazer pan of chafing dish. Heat over low flame, stirring occasionally, until ale just reaches the boiling point. Stir in lemon juice and soda. Mix well. Serve hot in mugs. Makes about 8 servings.

◄§ MENU §►

After Skating Snack

Spiced Ale
Pretzel Barrel

CIDER BOBBETS

2 quarts apple cider
¾ cup of sugar
6 whole cloves
1 stick cinnamon
8 spiced crab apples
1 cup rye whiskey

Beforehand Mix cider, sugar, and spices. Cover and let stand 1 hour. Marinate crab apples in whiskey for 1 hour.

Tray-Maid Spiced cider, marinated crab apples, and whiskey.

On Stage Place cider mixture in blazer pan of chafing dish and bring to a gentle boil. Lower heat and simmer 5 minutes. Add marinated apples and whiskey and heat 5 minutes longer. Serve each person with a bobbing apple. Makes 8 servings.

⊷§ MENU §⊶

Apple Bobbin for Grown-up Goblins
Date-Nut Bread Sandwiches
Cider Bobbets

SOUTH AMERICAN CHOCOFFEE

3 squares (3 ounces) unsweetened chocolate	1 teaspoon vanilla
	1½ cups strong hot coffee
1 quart light cream	1 cup brandy
1 cup sugar	1 cup heavy cream
dash salt	3 tablespoons powdered sugar

Beforehand   Break chocolate into small pieces. Just before starting, whip heavy cream with 3 tablespoons powdered sugar until mixture forms soft peaks.

Tray-Maid   Chocolate, cream, sugar, salt, vanilla, coffee, brandy, and whipped cream.

On Stage   Place chocolate, cream, sugar, and salt in blazer pan of chafing dish over hot water. Beat with a wire whisk until sugar is dissolved and chocolate is melted and well blended. Gradually beat in vanilla, coffee, and brandy. Just before serving, fold in whipped cream. Makes about 10 cups.

◦§   MENU   §◦

Drop in for After-Dinner Coffee

Special Sugared Pecans
Sherried Stuffed Prunes
South American Chocoffee

MEXICAN CHOCOLATE

2 cups strong black coffee
½ cup sugar
1½ tablespoons cornstarch
dash salt
2 squares (2 ounces) unsweet-
ened chocolate

1½ teaspoons ground cinna-
mon
1 teaspoon vanilla
3 cups light cream
1 jigger brandy
2 jiggers crème de cacao

Beforehand Mix sugar, cornstarch, and salt. Break chocolate into pieces. Mix cinnamon, vanilla, and cream.

Tray-Maid Coffee, sugar mixture, chocolate, flavored cream, brandy, and crème de cacao.

On Stage Place coffee, chocolate, and sugar mixture in blazer pan of chafing dish. Blend with a wire whisk until chocolate is melted and well blended and mixture is thickened (about 10 minutes). Gradually beat in flavored cream. Simmer, stirring occasionally, for 5 minutes, or until heated through. Just before serving, stir in brandy and crème de cacao. Makes 8 servings.

◄§ MENU §►

Progressive International Supper

(Last Course)

Fruit
Nut Meringue Cookies
Mexican Chocolate

HOT BURGUNDY CRANBERRY PUNCH

3 18-ounce cans cranberry juice
½ cup sugar
1 bottle burgundy
12 slices lemon
whole cloves

Beforehand   Stud lemon slices with whole cloves, using about 3 to a slice.

Tray-Maid   Cranberry juice, sugar, wine, and lemon slices.

On Stage   Place cranberry juice and sugar in blazer pan of chafing dish. Simmer 5 minutes, stirring occasionally, until sugar is dissolved. Add burgundy and simmer 5 minutes longer. Serve hot in mugs with slice of lemon. Makes about 12 servings, depending on size of mugs.

❧ MENU ☙

Trimming the Christmas Tree Party

Hot Burgundy Cranberry Punch
Frosted Doughnuts

HOT HAWAIIAN PUNCH WITH FRUIT KABOBS

2 18-ounce cans pineapple-
   grapefruit juice
2 sticks cinnamon
¼ cup sugar
¼ cup lemon juice

1 bottle sweet sauterne
1 13½-ounce can pineapple
   chunks
12-14 maraschino cherries
12-14 picks

Beforehand Mix sugar and lemon juice. Drain pineapple chunks and place 2 chunks on each pick with a cherry between.

Tray-Muid Fruit juice, cinnamon, sugar-lemon mixture, wine, and kabobs.

On Stage Simmer pineapple-grapefruit juice and cinnamon in blazer pan of chafing dish for 10 minutes. Remove cinnamon. Stir in sugar-juice mixture and heat until sugar dissolves. Add wine and simmer 5 minutes longer. Serve punch hot with a kabob in each cup. Makes 12-14 servings, depending on size of cups.

❦ MENU ❧

Patio Party

Finger Sandwiches
Assorted Relishes
Kidney Bean Salad
Hot Hawaiian Punch with Fruit Kabobs

MULLED WINE

1 bottle claret
1½ cups ruby port
½ cup apricot brandy
1 lemon, thinly sliced
1 orange, thinly sliced
3 cinnamon sticks, broken into pieces
6 whole cloves

Beforehand   Combine all ingredients in blazer pan of chafing dish and cover. Let stand for 1 hour.

Tray-Maid   Wine mixture.

On Stage   Place blazer pan over low heat. Bring wine mixture just to the boiling point, stirring constantly. Serve hot with slices of fruit. Makes 8-10 servings.

⊷ MENU ⊶
Anniversary Open House

Cheese Straws
Stuffed Celery
Salted Nuts
Stuffed Dates
Mulled Wine

AFTER-SKI PUNCH (SWEDISH GLUG)

1 bottle claret
1 cup 100-proof vodka
8 cardamon seeds
5 whole cloves
1 cup blanched almonds

1 cup seedless rasins
¼ cup chopped candied orange peel
1 cup cube sugar

Beforehand   Combine all ingredients except sugar in blazer pan of chafing dish. Cover and let stand 1 hour.

Tray-Maid   Wine mixture.

On Stage   Place blazer pan over low heat. Slowly bring wine mixture to a boil. Simmer 10 minutes. Put sugar in a large sieve and place over the hot wine. Ladle some of the liquor over the sugar and ignite. Continue to pour liquor over sugar until sugar is completely dissolved. Serve hot, being sure that each serving has almonds and raisins. Makes 10-12 servings.

❧   MENU   ☙

Fireside Punch Party

Swiss Cheese Twists
Pickled Mushrooms
Pot Cheese   Crackers
After-Ski Punch

Index